MW01248864

Gideon's Cry

Ben Barnhart

Gideon's Cry

Published by Streetlights Publications

Copyright © 2018 Benjamin C. Barnhart

Cover design by Austin John Rossborough

All rights reserved. Except for brief excerpts for review purposes, no part of this book may be reproduced in any form without written consent of the publisher.

All scripture quotations are taken from *The Holy Bible, New International Version®, NIV®*. Copyright © 1973, 1978, 1984 by Biblica, Inc.® Used by permission. All rights reserved worldwide.

ISBN: 0692177566
ISBN-13: 978-0692177563

GRATITUDE

First, my deepest thanks to everyone who read this manuscript at any stage and offered comments and encouragement: Mom, Dad, Liz, Justin, Brian, Dillon, Dave, Austin, Jeff, Sarah, J.R., and anyone else I may have forgotten. Thank you for sharing this road and helping me give voice to the cry in my heart.

Austin, thank you for your wonderful work on the cover design! You truly grasp the heart of the book and gave it an amazing visual expression.

Steve, thank you for the advice on how to make an actual book out of this and more importantly for helping me believe I could do it (and for asking if I was actually doing it!).

Liz, thank you for not giving up on me and for not letting me give up! Your encouragement sparked the rebirth of this project, and I never would have made it without you.

Ezra, thank you for making me want to live (and write about) a life worth passing down.

And finally, Jesus, Lord and Savior and Friend: All this is for you. May it be and do whatever you have in mind.

CONTENTS

Introduction

I believe in God. I began to as a child, but the process by which I've continued to believe into manhood has been complicated, and that's partially what this book is about. To clarify, I believe God is who he says he is in the Bible—the all-powerful creator who also somehow loves me and wants to meet with me, a friend and Lord, both supremely great and impossibly good. My belief and, more important, my experience of that greatness and love makes me want to live life however He leads. In this season of my life, that desire takes the shape of trying to grow up, leaving behind immaturity and becoming a man of God. I've been finding that it's a much longer and more challenging process than I was expecting it to be and that even at twenty-seven I often don't feel like a man.

I don't think I'm alone.

I have a suspicion that there are at least some of us, perhaps even a majority in my generation, who are profoundly discontent with the choices we're being offered about growing up, both within the church and outside of it. This book is first of all for those who feel the same way, those whose spirits cry out for something more than what people around them are doing. I'm no authority on the subject, but I am walking the same road. I'm journeying with all of you who are trying to become the men and women that God desires you to be, no matter the cost. My hope is that people of my generation may be encouraged in growing up by hearing some of my thoughts as I try to do the same.

Honestly, though, it doesn't matter how old you are. Maybe you're old enough that you've felt a cry burning in your heart for years, whether or not you know what to do with it. You might have even tried pretty hard to stifle it. This book is for you as well, if you're willing to risk it. If you'll be open to what's truly happening in your heart, who knows what God might show you? After all, we're all still growing up.

I'm sharing because stories are powerful, and I hope mine might offer a glimpse into what God might have for you as well. But don't take my word for it. If I could offer one suggestion on how to read this book, it would be to ask God himself if the things I'm saying about him are true. Use this as a springboard to dialogue with him. If it ends up doing nothing more than to get you talking with him, this book will be a success even if you never remember a word I say.

After all, I'm just one man with one story. I'm writing this specifically for people who are trying to grow up in the context of Christian community because that's the story I'm familiar with. I'm looking for my answers in God and his Word, but I have a feeling that the questions are still the same no matter where you look for answers. If you're growing up outside the church, this book is for you too because, frankly, the church has in many cases become so weak and ineffective that I can't blame you for thinking that we church people aren't any more likely than you to have the answers. Maybe if you take the time to read this, though, you'll find that what's going on in the Bible is worth looking into.

Speaking of the Bible, there are actually quite a few stories in there about people who were struggling to grow up. One in particular is found in the book of Judges, chapters 6-8, and reading it first (seriously, go ahead—my words can wait) will greatly help you to understand the rest of this book. It's about a man named Gideon.

PART I

When the angel of the Lord appeared to Gideon, he said, "The Lord is with you, mighty warrior."

"But sir," Gideon replied, "if the Lord is with us, why has all this happened to us? Where are all his wonders that our fathers told us about..."

Judges 6:12-13a

1. When the Lord Appeared

When God came to him, Gideon was threshing wheat in a winepress. Those are easy words to read and pass right over for someone (like me) who has never even seen a winepress, much less threshed any wheat. Here are two important facts, then, for people like me. First, a winepress is a small sunken area with walls just high enough for a man to hide in it, meant for collecting juice from grapes. Second, wheat threshing is best done in a large open area. That changes the picture.

Given that information, the only thing that explains the situation is fear. Gideon was in the winepress because he was afraid. The enemies of Israel had him (and the whole nation) so terrorized with the threat of taking everything from their crops to their very lives that he was willing to slowly and painfully attempt to separate wheat from chaff in a small area with very limited access to the wind that would make the task doable, and all that just to keep himself hidden.

That image reminds me of my generation. We may not live in a country under the occupation of our enemies—or then again, we might. It certainly doesn't seem that the prevailing values of American culture would encourage us to devote our lives to becoming the men and women God wants us to be. America has been hijacked by the idea that we should grow up to be who *we* want to be. To grow up according to that plan, we have to learn how to provide for ourselves, to get ours and protect it against a whole fleet of people just like us who are doing the same thing. We don't have the luxury of knowing who the enemy is: it could be anyone. The whole thing is very overwhelming.

In short, we are afraid, and we're being taught to live small. Small might seem like a strange word since the whole force of the secular establishment is pushing us towards more money, bigger stuff and greater indulgence. That's really just the packaging of the product, though. The real thing people are after is just safety and, having obtained that, whatever pleasure they can squeeze out of a short life in a hostile world. Small thinking hiding behind big talk and misdirection—it's like an English muffin pizza in an extra-large size box.

Shouldn't there be something more satisfying than that? It seems like the church, of all places, should be a setting where the misguided and futile nature of these pursuits is understood and an alternative plan (maybe God's true plan, even) is offered.

To some extent, it is. I don't mean to bash the church unnecessarily. I serve at a church that I love, and we (in our own imperfect way) are trying to address these problems. I think the American church in general has gotten soft, though. All too often, our alternative to the dangerous and ubiquitous selfishness of secular media and culture is just a diet soda to the world's regular: a sweeter, faker, less obviously harmful rehash of the same thing. Maybe we make the tiny pizza low-fat and gluten-free—but it's still tiny (plus it tastes worse).

What I mean to say is that we in the church sometimes try to solve the problems we see in secular culture by addressing only the blatantly sinful means by which that culture attempts to attain its goals. It's easy to quote Scriptures about avoiding greed, hedonism, selfishness and the like and feel as if that will solve the problem, but the thinking is still way too small. That kind of diet Christian-cola may not make us fat, but it will leave us thirsty because it's not water—the unsatisfying values it strives for remain the same.

Even in the church, we are sadly still often taught to value safety and pleasure, just to obtain them by different means (sound doctrine, moral living, everything in moderation, etc.). We can begin to feel that safety and pleasure are our purpose, when in fact they are completely beyond our control. Our best efforts to obtain them can be erased in a moment. Yet it is still so easy to devote our lives to getting them, even if by more morally sterile strategies than the world uses.

We don't want to be greedy—we just want to make enough to live in a nice house in a safe neighborhood no more than a twenty-minute drive from our work and church and a good school for our kids. We don't want to be impure, so we don't watch all the shows or movies, just the ones without most of the "really bad stuff." We don't want to be wrong, so we focus on knowing all the right doctrines at the expense of doing any of them.

We don't want that much wheat, just a nice little winepress where we can thresh out a little bit in hiding from a hostile world, enough to make some nice homemade bread and wait out this life so we can go to Heaven.

How in the world does that make sense? It only makes sense if you're afraid.

It turns out that the mission Jesus is actually calling his church to do is dangerous. He wants people who will go out into all the world and teach people how to follow him, engaging the real problems of a fallen culture with his love on the way, giving out cups of cold water in his name. His goals don't necessarily have anything to do with our safety and pleasure in this life—in fact, they might be extremely detrimental to those worldly values sometimes, and we're afraid of that.

Long story short, we find ourselves at the bottom of a winepress covered in chaff.

The only reason I've ever been taught for that scenario happening to Gideon was his own fear. I'm sure he was afraid, and I'm not saying that reason is invalid. I guess I just find it highly unlikely that a young guy like Gideon came up with the whole winepress threshing plan himself. He probably learned it from some older folks who were just as afraid as he was! If no one around you was aiming for anything better, you might be content with a life like that too.

That's one reason why growing up in the church can be so confusing. Becoming a man is already scary, and everyone seems to have adopted the safety and pleasure plan out of fear, as if there's no possibility for anything better. That sure doesn't seem like the plan Jesus was following and teaching! To do what he did (a life of service, no place to lay his head, the man of sorrows, crucifixion, etc.), you have to be extremely sure that there's something much better and more worth living for than your own physical safety and pleasure. You can't just quote a scripture about God's love—you have to believe it deep down in your guts to live a life as big as Jesus did. He fully lived out the good news he came to bring, a great part of which is that God's love and grace mean we don't have to live such small and fearful lives.

No more beating around the bush: the American Dream is nothing more than threshing wheat in a winepress. What vision is God calling us to instead?

2. The Lord Is With You

Down there in the winepress, Gideon probably didn't feel like God was with him at all. If I were him, I would have been feeling alone and hating it.

Actually, I've spent a lot of time alone in my life. Growing up as an only child is just like that, and it has its benefits and drawbacks just like any other birth order position or whatever the correct term is. I never used to mind being alone, though. Maybe it was because I knew my parents at least were never that far away, even when they needed a break from me or when I was off in my own little world of imaginary pursuits. I've always been very easily amused; maybe I didn't really notice any real problems. Maybe I just had the simple faith of a child that God was there and I'd be fine. I don't know.

Whatever the case, it all started changing recently. Especially when I moved out of my parents' house, but even before then, I started being uneasy in alone times. Increasingly, I filled them up with noise of various forms. These included everything from the outright sinful (e.g. pornography) to the simply worthless (YouTube) to the seemingly pious (an extensive prayer list). This was working for a while (easily amused, remember?), but then the various distractions I had been using started losing their power to keep my mind from the uneasiness that came in the silence. I felt like something was supposed to be happening in my life, something big, but I didn't know what it was or how to make it happen.

Ironically, I was running from the place where I could find those things out. I didn't know it, but I think that the internal pressure I felt (which certainly included the prodding and conviction of the Holy Spirit) was getting confused with some external pressure from the world and its idea of manhood.

According to the world system (at least as I felt it), you get spit out of college with the expectation that you should just be able to support yourself and figure out what you're doing and what you want to be. If you can't, then you go back to more college and dig a deeper hole, hoping that you find a ladder down there to get you out and on your feet at the end. In any event, the whole thing is completely up to you: finding your own way, making huge decisions you feel unequipped for, and of course paying for all of it.

It's really no wonder that so many people my age end up living in their parents' basements for years and years. It seems like a very logical choice. If we don't feel we can handle the world outside, we can at least put off the time when we have to do so. In the meantime, we can hide alone below ground level and do just enough to scrape by until something (hopefully) miraculously changes.

Hey, wait… that sounds a lot like threshing wheat in a winepress again.

That's pretty much what I was doing. Not in my parents' basement, thankfully—there are big centipedes down there. My room was upstairs. But yeah, pretty much the same story. I thought moving out would solve the problem and get me started on my own. As it turns out, you can easily change your physical location without addressing the underlying problem of growing up.

As far as I see it, there are only two ways out of this situation: the one I used to be trying, and the one I'm trying now. The first is to become an expert at fudging things. This is the "fake it till you make it" strategy, and some people seem to eventually end up doing things they enjoy and are fit for (i.e. become independent men/women) using it. I'm not sure if or how this really happens, but it seems to.

The other way is to realize that you don't have to become a man or woman alone.

There is somebody with you who sees the whole situation. Even better, this person is powerful enough to set you up anywhere he pleases. Better yet, he actually has planned a place in his extensive network of connections to plug you into. He is also perfectly willing to speak to you about the whole thing, and you don't have to leave him endless voicemails or résumés or go through his annoying secretary to get there.

There is one potential problem, though. His voice can be fairly still and small. In order to hear it, silence is required—the same silence that feels unbearable due to all the pressure building up from all over the place.

If you hang around a church long enough, you'll probably hear somebody talk about the value of silence. They might even call it a "spiritual discipline," which is just a fancy way of saying you really ought to do it, and if you already are doing it, you should do it an undefined amount more. Nothing like adding the feeling of moral failure and guilt to help a difficult and confusing situation, right?

But it's not about guilt—it's about faith. You know, at any time during the past months and years as I've been trying to grow up, if you had asked me if I believed that God was real and powerful and could actually speak to me, I would have said yes. My brain would have assented that it was true. But obviously I didn't really believe it, because I wasn't being quiet enough to give him a chance. These days, I'm starting to believe it.

Like it or not, silence is key to this whole process. What I didn't understand, but have been learning recently, is that it's not the end but the means. The point is not some zen-like state where we try to merge our thought into nothingness. The point is that life is meant to be a conversation and we don't know how to listen. If you try to have a face-to-face talk with your significant other while blasting your music and staring at your phone every moment you aren't the one speaking, he or she might not feel you are terribly significant for much longer, if you catch my drift. But we do that to God all the time. We talk to him (if we even spend much time doing that), and then we turn the noise back on. Plain and simple, it's rude.

So silence is really just about relationship. It's about giving God his turn in the conversation. It's not about trying to make something happen, just about being with a real person and being truly present in real life. A real thing about me: I love anagrams, moving the letters of words around to make new ones. Guess what you can make out of silent: *listen*.

If you decide to be quiet and try listening to God, I predict some things will start happening. They did for me, anyway. First, you might feel like you're going to panic if you end up all alone in the silence. You might actually panic and give up. If you keep trying, though, it might start to seem peaceful (a hallmark of the presence of God). I recommend trying to listen in different places, by the way. Being alone in silence in a dimly lit room could be depressing—so take a walk. Go to the beach, or wherever works.

Something else you might feel is happening during times of silence is absolutely nothing. That is totally normal and understandable—just like your best friends are the ones you can just hang out around without having to talk all the time, God simply wants to be with you. He is happy when you take the time, and it's not all about getting something done, whatever that means. Even in times when you don't feel anything happen, though, just setting your heart consciously in the presence of God has some powerful effects. You might not notice it at the time, but it's like you're soaking a sponge in good, clean water. Then when life squeezes you in some way or another, you suddenly find that good things come out in ways that surprise even you. When that happens, you won't have to look any further for the reason than those times of silence.

One last thing I predict will happen if you'll be silent is that God will speak. It probably won't be an audible voice, although I wouldn't rule that out. I've never heard that. But maybe in your heart, you'll start to realize he really is there. Maybe you'll feel his direction and affirmation start to wash away the overwhelming stress of figuring it out yourself, like Gideon did. Or you might just come face to face with the beautiful and unimaginable fact that the God of the entire universe loves you—so much that he died to bring you back to him out of whatever winepress you've been hanging out in. Who knows what could happen if you start hearing and believing that? I've been starting to, and it's bringing me alive, giving me the hope to continue. Despite the sin and fear and mess and noise, God really does want to be with us.

By the way, it doesn't really matter if you believe he can do this or not when you start trying to listen—as long as you start. God didn't stop to check if Gideon believed he could speak to him. He just spoke.

He was with him.

He's still here, and he's still speaking. What does he want to say?

3. Mighty Warrior

God first told Gideon that he was with him, ready to speak. The very next thing God wanted to share was Gideon's true identity as a man. In what has to be one of the most unexpectedly encouraging votes of confidence ever, God named Gideon a mighty warrior.

Gideon completely ignored him.

Later on, Gideon would come up with some reasons why God was probably wrong about him, but at this point he let those incredible words fly right over his chaff-covered head and out of the winepress. It seems he wasn't convinced of God's true identity yet, so he didn't even think of disputing his own. He countered God's blessing first with doubts about who God was: if you're with us, shouldn't things be better?

We'll look more at these doubts soon, but for now just take a second and think about how ludicrous it is that Gideon immediately resisted and argued against God's blessing. Even if he was skeptical, wouldn't he have wanted to believe what had been said with everything in him? Why in the world did he try to shot-block God's blessing like that?

And why do I do the exact same thing?

Now in fairness to Gideon, he may not have figured out yet that he was speaking to God himself. This seems to have dawned on him rather suddenly after the messenger to whom he'd been speaking caused the food Gideon offered to be consumed by fire that came out of a rock. Oh, and then the guy disappeared. Perhaps Gideon wouldn't have argued so much if he had seen that first. I, on the other hand, don't have any such excuse.

The Bible is full of God's affirmations of our identity as believers in Jesus. We are God's children, co-heirs of his kingdom, a royal priesthood, a people set apart for specific exploits that God has planned to do through us, and any number of other callings so amazing that words really can't do them justice. We would never say any of these things aren't true, but many of us may try to subtly temper God's expectations of us. We may find ourselves leading fairly ordinary, lower middle-class types of lives that don't seem terribly amazing. The danger, then, is that we only ask God (or believe him) for the middle-class version of the promises.

I don't say that to diminish the value of the normal everyday things we do, because all of these can become worship to God when done with the right heart. In fact, many things we think of as ordinary (raising children, being a faithful worker, caring for aging parents, etc.) should really be transferred into the amazing exploits category if you ask me. My point is not that these things are lesser or smaller. My point is that I know I tend to settle for what I'm sure I can handle on my own at the expense of even asking what God might be calling me to do or be instead.

For me, this takes the form of a very strange mix of pride and fear. At least I've always thought of it as strange, but the more I vocalize it and share it with others, the more I see how it is common to all of us. Pride and fear may actually be two sides of the same coin. If I wasn't setting myself in a high place through pride, I wouldn't have to fear being knocked down.

Let me describe how I've seen this paralyzing mixture work in my life. For whatever set of dysfunctional reasons (probably at least partially an only child thing again), I have grown up thinking I could do just about anything—and not just do it, but do it better than everyone else (or at least the great majority of them). God made me a fast learner and a quick thinker, but I'm not talking about an Eminem-like belief that I could do anything I set my mind to. I'm talking about irrationally thinking I can do all of it, whether I set my mind to it or not. If I ever did set my mind to something, of course I could immediately become the best in the world at it.

Needless to say, this is a very precarious belief upon which to base one's worldview. It threatens to topple at any moment, in fact. The only way to make sure you can keep on believing this lie is to try very few things—things you already know you're pretty good at and/or things where failure can be blamed on outside forces. You have to run from everything else, and this is what we commonly call fear.

Do you identify with responding in fear to anything that jeopardizes your pride? Do you want to believe you are all-powerful to the point that you're extremely frightened of being proved wrong? That's been my struggle. Maybe that's why I didn't learn to ride a bike till I was seventeen, for example. Having failed at it when I was about seven, I just moved it to the "things I can probably do but am afraid to try in case I can't" category—for a decade.

That is a prime example of why this kind of backward belief system makes growing up so hard. Becoming a man (or woman—though I'm probably not going to keep saying both for the whole book simply because I don't know anything about becoming a woman, although I believe that becoming a godly woman is just as hard and valuable as becoming a man and I'm sure a lot of the same lessons apply to both) is inherently risky. Trying to find your place seems to put your identity on the line, and the ways you can fail at it entail much more serious consequences than skinned knees.

At some point, you have to come face-to-face with the fact that there might be people better than you even at your treasured field of dominance. Imagine my dismay when I searched online to find out that my all-time best Minesweeper scores, far from being the greatest ever as I supposed, barely even cracked the top 500 in the world rankings (yes, there are world rankings for that)! I stopped playing for a year. Actually, that turned out to be a good decision, but it was still made for the wrong reasons.

Back to my point: imagine that same helpless feeling happening in something that actually matters, like trying to find a job. Why wouldn't the response be to stop trying? Or to stop believing God's promises? Or maybe just to sort of believe them, but only a little?

Gideon challenged God's promise first, not his own identity. Ever since I discovered the pride/fear paradigm I've been talking about, I've wondered if that wasn't exactly where Gideon found himself down in the winepress. Apparently, he was a pretty charismatic, gifted guy, as we'll see later. I would bet that he believed somewhere in himself that of course he had what it took to save Israel. Maybe he even daydreamed about it as he threshed the wheat in his tiny subterranean box. Maybe he was just afraid to try.

Whatever the case may be on that dramatic imputation of my own feelings to a biblical character, I think the truth still remains that Gideon doubted himself because he doubted

God. He ignored the name of mighty warrior because he didn't really believe God was with him.

I know this is going a bit out of order storywise, but look at the reasons he gave when he did finally get around to saying why he wasn't the mighty warrior God was looking for (Judges 6:15, if you're the kind of person who follows all the directions of authors). They're all comparisons: my family is weak, I'm the youngest one, basically there are any number of people more qualified than me to do this. That sounds just like running in fear from something that might set one up for a humiliating failure.

All our pride (and shame) is rooted in comparisons just like that: I'm more of a man than this person, but less of one than this other guy. Maybe I can do this thing God called me to, but it sure looks like someone else would have a better shot at it. I think I just might be able to save Israel, but I'd rather thresh wheat in a winepress than be the one that tried and failed to do it.

What Gideon needed to (and would grow to) understand, and what God has also been helping me see, is this: comparisons are irrelevant in God's kingdom.

In fact, they're a big waste of time. For one thing, all they do is bring us down because (contrary to what I believed) no one can be the best at everything—or even have the highest overall score on some imaginary metric of goodness. More important, no matter where we think we stack up compared to anyone else in any category, only one person knows who we really are. God created us, and he knows the end from the beginning. If he says we are something (a mighty warrior, for example), what authority could be higher than that? There's no point in ranking ourselves on any scale along with the rest of our peers. God has individual plans for each of us regardless of what we see as our qualifications. He qualifies us and that's it.

By the way, the time I did finally learn to ride a bike was a moment of clarity where I understood this thing I'm talking about. Our church's youth group, which I was leading at the time, was doing a bike-a-thon to raise money for our new building, and I knew God wanted me to help, even though I also knew every single one of the kids I was leading would be a better rider than me. Somehow he showed me that it didn't matter because he had chosen me as the leader and what they thought made no difference. So I borrowed a bike and teetered around a parking lot alone until I thought I could handle going twenty-six miles with everyone else. Long story short, I made it, but yes, I did crash that bike in front of all those kids (twice actually, but once was because one of them shot me with a pellet gun, so I didn't count that. He got stung by a bee later in the ride, which I considered divine justice). I didn't care. I had done what God asked me to do.

Understanding God's nature as the One who couldn't possibly care less about our earthly qualifications will help us move past our silly comparisons and the pride and fear they cause. Our self-doubt, like Gideon's, is not the root problem, but it can point us to the real issue: we doubt God, so we don't experience the freedom of knowing He loves us. As I look back on my bike-riding story, I wonder why more of my life hasn't been marked by that kind of freedom. Why do I hardly ever feel like a mighty warrior?

I have a feeling it's because I still tend to doubt God. What identity could I step into if I didn't?

4. But Sir...

Whatever else we might want to say about Gideon, he was a man ready with an answer. In this case, it wasn't really a good answer, but still. He lost no time in disputing his visitor's claim that God was with him—and in so doing, he totally missed the point.

The Bible doesn't tend to indicate the pauses that naturally happen in conversation, so maybe Gideon stopped to think before he said what he said. It sure seems like it was right on the tip of his tongue, though. I like to think he was a thoughtful type of guy (like me) who tended to get distracted by deep thoughts even while he was supposed to be working. Maybe he had been pondering God's seeming abandonment of Israel the whole time he was threshing.

I've always read the story like that was true, and it reminds me of one of my favorite moments from the Sherlock Holmes stories I loved so much as a kid (and still do). In one of them, Holmes and his friend Dr. Watson are sitting together in silence in their parlor, which is what British people like to call their living rooms. By intently watching the progress of Watson's eyes around the room, Holmes is able to interject an answer to the very question Watson is silently pondering, to which Watson instantly agrees before realizing with a shock what has just happened. I've always wanted to do a thought interception like this to one of my friends, but alas, Sherlock Holmes, being fictional, has a much easier time with those kinds of things than I.

Anyway, my point in all that is that God anticipated Gideon right at the point of his doubts. He doubted himself, as we saw in the last chapter, but more importantly he doubted whether God was really with Israel at all. When God spoke, "The Lord is with you, mighty warrior," he brought both of these doubts front and center. Because he is God, it is highly unlikely that this was an accident.

Basically, God pulled a Sherlock Holmes on him, and he fell for it just like Dr. Watson. Unlike Holmes, though, who just used his abilities to show off, God had a specific purpose in mind in addressing Gideon's deepest and as yet unvocalized thoughts.

It's pretty safe to infer that whatever God leads off a conversation with is the first thing that needs to be addressed. God doesn't tend to start with "Hey, what's up?" or anything like that. If you want proof, what did He say to the group of terrified disciples he appeared to after the resurrection? "Peace be with you." If you want more, check out his interventions in the lives of Saul on the road to Damascus, Elijah hiding on Mount Horeb, Adam and Eve after they sinned or pretty much any other time he said anything to anyone in the whole Bible. God always tells people exactly what they need to hear to achieve his purpose.

So apparently, Gideon's doubts needed to be challenged in order for things to move forward. That leaves me with the question of why that was the place to start, and not just because I want to understand the story better. If Gideon's doubt was so serious, what is mine doing to me?

One reason our doubt of God is such a big deal is that it actually blinds us to reality. If Jesus is the truth incarnate, any doubt of him is a failure to see life the way it really is. It's just that it's pretty hard to see the problem when it's in your own eye. A friend of mine recently had cataract removal surgery on both of his eyes, and I happened to see him in the few days between getting the first eye done and the second. The eye that had already been fixed was noticeably clearer than the other, which looked like it had some type of white cloud in it. He told me he had hardly noticed as this cloudiness settled gradually on both his eyes until he started needing to have his wife read him road signs as they drove! Only once one eye was fixed did he realize what he had been missing.

From my experience, that's exactly how doubt works. Little by little, our unbelief takes us to places where we don't want to be and keeps us from seeing the way to get back home. For Gideon, it already had him down in a winepress hiding to start off with. Even more startling, his reply of doubt was so ready on his tongue that he seems to have completely missed the fact that he was speaking directly to the Lord! The Truth himself stood before Gideon, and he didn't even see it at first.

I wonder sometimes how much my doubts about God's ability and willingness to provide for my future (i.e. his power and his love) might be causing me to miss what God is doing in my life. Thankfully, God is faithful to keep working to get the obstacle of doubt out of our way, and every now and then he does cataract surgery on us, so to speak. In the most recent one of these for me, God showed me how much I'd been focusing on my own plans for becoming a man at the expense of his plans to build his kingdom through me.

It makes a lot of sense that doubt would work that way. As the world around us gets more and more blurry, we tend to focus on what is closest to us, and what could be closer than ourselves? We stop being able to see past the ends of our own noses, as Mary Poppins would put it. That's why self-doubt is such a logical outgrowth of the root of God-doubt. The more we look away from God and at ourselves, the more clearly we see how incompetent we are to produce the results we know God is asking us for. The goal, be it saving a nation or just becoming a man, starts looking impossible.

As an example, take the apostle Peter, who was literally walking on top of water to Jesus when doubt entered his mind. He looked down at his feet to see if he was really doing what he seemed to be doing. As soon as he shifted his focus from Jesus to himself, he realized, "hey, I can't actually walk on water!" Then he started to sink.

But he *was* walking on water before he looked. And Jesus, whose power was supporting him as he did, never started sinking the whole time. Peter's doubt just blinded him to that reality.

As I look at myself, I realize that I don't even really know exactly what it means to become a man of God. I've been trying to solve that problem by figuring out what it means. The only way to actually solve it, though, is to start looking somewhere else.

Maybe that's why God seems to answer so many of my prayers for specific future direction by simply leading me to worship him. My prayers for a job, a wife, stability, etc. reveal more than just my desires—they also reveal my doubts that God will provide. His answer, then, is to lead me before his throne in worship, where I can see clearly how able he is to provide anything in the world, and how much he loves me. Worship is the laser surgery that opens my eyes to the true reality of life: the all-powerful and loving God who runs the show.

God used worship to open Gideon's eyes too. As he allowed Gideon to express his doubts through prayer, Gideon began to realize that he was actually praying! He might be one of the only people ever to pray (i.e. talk with God) by accident, but it eventually dawned on him what might be happening, and he brought an offering to his visitor. When this offering spontaneously combusted, he realized how wrong and offensive all his unbelief had been and thought God was probably going to kill him.

He didn't, though. Shockingly, God accepted Gideon's offering and spared him even after his tantrum of doubts. In fact, this was the beginning of an elaborate process by which God systematically eviscerated all the doubt in Gideon's heart. He wanted Gideon to see the reality of his power and love in order to give him faith to accomplish what God was asking him to do. A big part of becoming a man is learning to see this as well.

Too often, I read God's promises in the Bible or feel him affirming my dreams for the future that I don't see yet, and the first word out of my mouth is "But…" just like it was for Gideon. If I were God, I don't think I would have any patience for that kind of whining, but Gideon did it and I do it, so I assume that people have been doing it to him throughout the thousands of intervening years as well. Yet even still, he allows us to speak our doubts and uses that as an opportunity to take the clouds from our eyes so we can see the truth again. Gideon, like me, tended to relapse into distrust after worship.

God kept pointing his eyes back to reality.

Even a prayer of doubt is still a prayer: a belief, maybe even just a hope, that God is there and has a better life for us than the one we see as doubt covers our eyes. If God had grace for Gideon's doubtful cry, we can believe that he will open our eyes as well if we just ask. As one of my favorite biblical prayers puts it, "Lord, I believe; help my unbelief."

We can come before God with anything, even our doubts. Why don't we?

5. Why?

Maybe one of the biggest reasons we don't come to God with our doubts and questions is that he always answers us on his own terms, not ours. It's impossible for us to throw him off the trail of his own purposes and get him onto our track in which we demand explanation. We desperately want to know the reasons for things (at least I do, and Gideon did), but God wants us to walk by faith, not sight.

The Bible clearly teaches that everything God does has a specific purpose (or multiple interrelated purposes). God is not random, nor does he get surprised by "coincidences." His sovereign plan bends every single thing that happens, even the evil he so hates, to ultimately accomplish his will for his people (Romans 8:28). We don't know exactly how he does this while honoring our free will, but all Christians accept in faith that he does. It's a paradox, but also orthodox. The mistake it can lead to, though, is thinking that because God has a purpose for everything, we should have the right to know that purpose—or at least be able to figure it out if we try hard enough.

It seems like I'm always asking God why. Why this, why that: Why can't I write better songs? Why are my teeth crooked? Why did you give me the desire to be a husband and father and then call me to be single for (what seems to me to be) such a long time? Why do Cleveland's sports teams always have to be so bad or else come agonizingly close to victory while falling just short?... and so on.

It's pretty much the least helpful question possible.

In many cases it is, at least. God is a very patient father, and he has never forbidden us to ask him why about anything we could possibly imagine. He just never promised that he would answer the question. If we think we deserve an explanation from him just because there is one—we don't. His ways are higher than ours, and we might not even understand if he told us. Maybe that's why he doesn't... and there I go again trying to figure it out. It kind of gets to be a vicious cycle.

It reminds me of a whole different stage in the process of growing up—a much earlier one. The way I see it, little kids learning to talk usually go through several distinct language phases. First is the nonsense phase, in which they have a lot to say and are saying it but have no idea that no one else is getting it. We must confuse these poor children horribly when we talk nonsense back to them—kind of a dirty trick if you ask me, making them think they're actually communicating. Second comes the phase of basic concepts. The first four basic concepts seem to be Mom, Dad, More and No. Often there is a heavy emphasis on the no. Any concepts added to the repertoire are then repeated endlessly. Right after this, though, usually concurrent with figuring out that "No!" as a constant response is not going to fly, comes the phase I'm talking about—you guessed it: "Why?"

As little kids, we believe that mom or dad or really any adult has the keys to the mysteries of the universe, and we have to get our hands on them. We especially want to know why we have to do things we don't want to do, but it can apply to just about anything. Maybe you've seen this cycle play out before: parent says something; child asks why. Parent gives logical reason, somehow thinking that will end the discussion. Far from it; child says why again. Lather, rinse, repeat. This can go on forever, or until the parent finally realizes that logic is not the answer because little kids (like us) know how to ask the questions long before they know how to understand the answers. When this realization strikes, the parent says something in a very final tone like "because I said so." In my house, it was "because I'm your *mother*, that's why!" End of discussion, but often a frustrating conclusion for both sides, as I recall.

It's that very cycle that God does his best to keep us out of. His standard response to the why question seems to be totally ignoring it. Note: we're leaving the parent analogy behind here.

I don't know how to solve the endless why cycle of the three-year-old, but I do not advocate ignoring your children. God doesn't ignore us either, when it comes down to it—just the question. For example, the Psalms are full of David's whys but very sparse on any answers God may or may not have given him. Yet God spoke many other things to him as he asked.

Another example of God's strategy with us is Job, who spent 37 chapters or so insistently asking God why and challenging him to defend himself for ruining Job's life. Meanwhile, Job's friends were playing the game I play and trying to explain God's thoughts and ways to him. When God finally responded to Job, he essentially said, "Who do you think you are to ask me why? Oh, and your friends are so far off the mark that I'm going to kill them if you don't pray for them." Sobering. Job did pray for them, but still. Then, as soon as he stopped asking why, God blessed him twice as much as before—but again without any explanation. That's just how he rolls.

God was less offended at the honest question than at the pretentious claims of the friends who thought they had all the answers. He still didn't answer it, though.

The same thing happened to Gideon. His syntax was a little more advanced, but his reply to God's mighty warrior blessing was still basically the standard three-year-old special: "But why?" God, however, easily brushed aside Gideon's attempt to control the situation. His reply (the subject of Part II of this book) has always struck me as having a hint of frustration, but it was nonetheless a reply of even further blessing. Really, God ignored Gideon's demand for explanation and answered the question he should have asked, which was *how*, not why.

That's what I should be asking too. It might not be so important on questions like why the Browns are always so bad, but what answers might God have for me if I started asking him how instead of why on the bigger questions? How can I work towards becoming a godly husband and father? How can I stop being lazy? How can I worship you more purely? How do I become a mighty warrior? How do I become a man? Those answers will be far more productive.

Honestly, if all we ever ask God is why, what does that say about our maturity? He is always gracious with us as spiritual toddlers, but his heart is that we grow up to be men and women of faith who will learn how to follow him without always knowing why he does what he does. As we do, we might find that we don't really want to have to understand the whole world.

It's a blessing, really, that we get to leave the understanding part to God. How long will it take us to accept this gift and start asking the right questions?

6. Where Are All the Wonders?

I'm hoping to learn quicker than he did, but at this point in the story Gideon still had a few more of the wrong questions to ask. His doubt was not a vague or general uneasiness but a list of very specific questions meant to prove the message God was sending him couldn't possibly be true.

After leading off with "But why did all this bad stuff happen?" Gideon moved on to challenge God's strength specifically. Basically, he asked, "If you're with us, shouldn't we be seeing some power and deliverance around here?"

Although I think this question was misguided on his part, there is something important that Gideon was getting at here. He was right in thinking that where God is, there will be power. Amazing things happen in his presence throughout Scripture; He is known as the God of Wonders (see Exodus 15:11).

This kernel of truth in Gideon's doubt is important because people—specifically young people—are still asking this kind of question today. They hear the church's claims of God's favor and the miraculous biblical stories, and then they look at the actual church and think, "So where are all the wonders?" If they don't see any, they're likely to give up on God as a possible source for the identity and fulfillment they so desperately seek.

At least, that's what I nearly did. Just as I was entering the phase of life often euphemistically called "becoming a man" (i.e. puberty, in case you never heard it called that), my family was involved in a church that was falling apart at the seams over some trivial issues. They did teach me to read the Bible there, though, and as I did I saw that the Christians in it did amazing things through God's power. Not only did they heal the sick and do other visible miracles, but they also had power to reach non-Christians with the message of salvation, and they loved each other with the love of God—each just as miraculous as any of the others if you ask me. Anyway, none of that seemed to be happening in that church.

Finally, when that church split down the middle, my family left. After that, the pastor and his wife (who stayed, of course) wouldn't let me see their son, who had been one of my best friends, anymore. A huge disconnect started to form in my mind. I believed in Jesus by this time, but if that was what his church was all about I wanted nothing to do with it. I knew what the Bible taught, but I didn't see it happening, so I was legitimately questioning whether any of it was real.

The most tragic thing about my story is that it isn't just mine. Nor is it just the story of an isolated few. This kind of thing happens in God's church all the time, where God's love is supposed to be shining and his will should be in effect the most. Even in solid churches, kids trying to become adults can find hypocrisy in parents who say one thing in the church and do another outside of it. Then of course there are the large-scale splits and needless divisions all too often. Where are the wonders?

The wrong answer to that question would be to assume that God is not with his church, as Gideon assumed God had left Israel. It's hard for me to blame kids with stories like mine who arrive at this conclusion, but God's heart is to rescue these hurting and confused children.

God rescued me by providing me with some new friends who invited me to a church (that I still attend) where, despite the occasional mess and struggle that comes with being human, people really do love each other and fight for unity. What's more, they also prayed for me and things started to happen. The Holy Spirit, who I learned was already inside me because I had trusted in Christ, started to speak to my heart. I found out I had spiritual gifts, a concept that had been completely left out of the doctrines my previous Sunday school teachers had drilled into my head. My new friends prayed for sick people believing God could heal, loved their Christian family and reached out to those outside it with power. All the things I had read and learned about started to click into place once I saw them being acted out. It was wonderful.

Unfortunately, many people I know don't have a redemption story like mine. God has been very gracious to me in keeping me from walking away from his truth, but what is his heart for those who do turn their back on him because of the hypocrisy or weakness of his people?

Quite simply, he wants to show them his wonders.

That's what he was about to do for Gideon in the story, despite his doubts and disrespect. Gideon was about to witness (and get to take part in) a series of increasingly unbelievable displays of God's power that brought him back to full trust in the Lord. But first, he had to get out of the winepress.

The winepress, as I offered in chapter 1, is where I believe the American church too often resides. God doesn't change, so he is still the God of wonders. If we aren't seeing them, the fault does not lie with God. The fault could, however, lie with a bunch of his followers living life in a scared, self-centered underground world of our own making. The view just isn't very good from down there.

Although God is doing a lot of amazing things in and through my church and many other great individual churches I know of, we still need God's power desperately. In the larger picture, the church as a whole is not looking like a tremendously wondrous place to me these days. Too many Christians are so caught up in chasing safety and pleasure in our man-made boxes of security and seclusion that we forget about our great need for God. Therefore, we far too rarely see God's supernatural power to heal, save and love.

That power is the only way the present wandering generation of would-be adults can be rescued.

I say all this not to affix any blame, but as a challenge to myself and to anyone else who wants to take it. If I'm not seeing the wonders I believe are necessary to save a generation of people like me desperately searching for identity and manhood, who needs to get out of the winepress?

I do.

I might not be able to change the church as a whole. I might not even be able to push my own individual church in the right direction. But by God's grace, I can leave behind my little subterranean boxes of fear and self-centeredness where I've threshed out such a small crop. I can value a life of risky devotion to God and the search for his wonders over the fleeting defenses and distractions of this world. I can give up my own time and money to pursue the ones wandering from God and tell them about the hope and love I've found. I can promote unity in the church instead of discord. Through it all,

I can come to God with my doubts and pursue him unswervingly until he changes me by his grace.

There is no other way. I could sit around like Gideon bemoaning the bad things that have happened to me. I could wonder if God has left his church, like Gideon wondered if God had left Israel. Or I could get out of the winepress and maybe see some of the amazing things God wants to do and is already doing! God, being who he is, certainly has a place for me to participate.

I can move towards being a man of God as I get out of my winepress and see His wonders. Why am I still so concerned with my own safety and self that I don't do it?

7. Our Fathers Told Us

If there is one main reason we get preoccupied with providing for our own safety, it's that we don't understand the love of our Father.

I'm talking about God our Father when I say that, not our earthly fathers. It is foundational to our lives to know that, no matter what we do or say or how we fail or succeed at manhood or life in general, we are the children of the King. We are adopted brothers of Christ himself if we accept his sacrifice on our behalf, and God is not in the business of disowning his sons for any reason. In fact, he's only done it once, and that was to Jesus, who carried all our sins on the cross to guarantee it wouldn't happen to us. Then he was raised into glory where he now intercedes on our behalf. It's unbelievably good news.

So why don't we get it? I mean, as Christians we say we do, but why don't we live in the full implications of this truth? If we really believed that no failure, no matter how severe, could change our core identity as beloved sons even the tiniest bit, would we be so concerned about safety?

My guess is that we don't walk in the full security of having God as our Father largely because we have earthly fathers that are broken, sinful people. On top of that, a lot of them are still trying to figure out manhood themselves since their fathers were the same way! I now understand that being a man is not something you suddenly just get when you reach a certain age. There's a generational cycle of brokenness fueled by sin that keeps us from understanding the love we were meant to live in.

If we assume (consciously or unconsciously) that God is like our human fathers, which we tend to do, then we open ourselves up to all manner of different mistaken beliefs about the character of God. For example, some people have abusive fathers. Is God like that, punishing and raging at any time for no discernible reason? He isn't, of course, but you can see how a boy receiving the scars of that upbringing would ask the question and possibly begin believing in the unseen depths of his heart that the God who runs a world where that can happen is the same way.

What if your father left your family, or died when you were young? Although one of those options is a sinful choice and one is completely beyond control, both could send the message to a child that at any moment their protection could be snatched away, so they'd best learn to protect themselves. Fathers who are intentionally absent add the crippling weight of rejection to the mix as well, making their children wonder if they're even worth protecting.

These are fairly extreme (although unfortunately still all too common) examples used to make the point that our fathers can profoundly influence our views of God. Even the best fathers will still be sinful people, mixed bags of good and bad traits that can produce warped views of God.

Take Gideon's father, for instance. Apparently, he had done part of what God commanded by telling his son about the wonders God had done for Israel in the past. In doing so, he at least gave Gideon a fragmentary understanding of a God who fought on his side in love and had the power to back it up. However, Gideon's father also had an altar to a pagan god in his yard alongside a (probably pornographic) statue of a fertility goddess. Talk about a mixed message!

It's really no wonder, then, that Gideon was racked by doubts about God's identity. If his father truly believed the stories of God's wonders he was telling, then why would he need the pagan gods as well? And why would he have his son hiding from their enemies in a winepress?

If that example still seems a bit extreme, let me tell you some of my own story. God has blessed me with one of the greatest fathers you could ask for. He taught me the Bible, led me to trust in Jesus, and devoted countless hours to my growth and development in many ways. But he's still just a man. Despite how much he loves me, his brokenness still caused me to view God in a twisted way for many years.

One time in the seventh grade, I brought back a report card from school. I was home-schooled through the fifth grade, so I had only one year of report cards under my belt at the time, but they'd all been good. On this particular day, the card I brought home had six A's on it... and one B. It was a B+, I think, but it was the first one I'd ever gotten. It was for Art.

I was thinking, "Who cares about that—it doesn't have anything to do with how smart I am!" and I was excited to show off another sterling academic record. When I showed it to my dad, though, he took one look at it and before saying anything else asked, "What happened here with this B?"

I was devastated. It seemed logically to me like six A's should outweigh that. I'm not sure if he was joking or not, but the effect was still the same. We've talked about it since, and he doesn't remember this even happening, so he clearly wasn't deliberately trying to send me a message. It still produced the fruit, though, that I began to think I needed to be perfect in order to be accepted as a son.

Perfection, as you may know, is a very heavy burden to carry through life, and it only gets heavier as you reach the uncertainty and unavoidable mistakes of becoming a man. It's a lesson that God has had to repeatedly unteach me over the years, yet I learned it from a man who by any reasonable standard is one of the best fathers you could ever have.

Do you see a common thread running through these examples? I do—fear. The brokenness of our fathers causes us to misunderstand God in ways that make us afraid. If we're abused, we fear that God is vengeful and unpredictable. If we're abandoned, we fear that God may take his protection from us at any moment (or that he isn't strong enough to protect us in the first place). If our fathers serve other gods, we'll be afraid that the one true God isn't enough to deal with our problems. Even good fathers that want to challenge us to be our best can make us afraid that God won't accept us unless we're perfect.

Similarly, in God's church, if we don't see enough godly men (spiritual fathers) walking down the path of life and strength that is biblical manhood, we'll be afraid that there's nothing more ahead of us than a life devoted to scrambling for our own safety and any pleasure we can somehow eke out.

This pattern makes a lot of sense when you think about it. The only thing that drives out fear is perfect love (1 John 4:18). Our fathers can't give us that, of course, because they aren't perfect. So instead, we inherit from them fear and mistrust of God. And again, this can lead us into a variety of winepress-type situations. Thankfully, there is a way out, and it's the same for us as it was for Gideon: divine intervention.

Despite all the mixed messages Gideon received and the fear he lived in, God just came and talked to him. He's still doing this today. No one knows better than he does how damaged we've been by our own fathers, and no one can tell us the truth of who God is better than God. Even better, he's given us his Word in the Bible, which is full of affirmations of our identity as his sons through unconditional love. As Christians, he has even given us his Spirit to speak these truths personally and directly into our hearts as we pray and read.

If that sounds too easy or too good to be true, I challenge you just to ask God about it. If it's something you desire but don't see, ask him to prove it to you—to show you it's true in such a way that you can feel it and believe it. As we'll see later, Gideon did that and God came through for him. And I feel confident in God's ability to rise to any challenge because he has started speaking these things to me in ways that are totally revolutionizing the way I live life.

For example, I started praying for God to show me his love, and within weeks my dad and mom both came to me asking for forgiveness for the ways they sinned against me as a kid and the wrong beliefs it caused. We've been able to talk about all this stuff and work through it, and in forgiving them (and asking their forgiveness for some of how I treated them too), God has brought untold blessing and peace to my life.

God also led me to read a book called *The Prodigal God* by Timothy Keller, which I highly recommend. As I read it, God spoke powerfully to me the truth that, through faith in his grace, I am God's son no matter what, and his welcome to me is extravagant and never-ending. Ever since then, I've been living in more freedom because who cares about the little things that can go wrong when the most important thing, being his son, can never go wrong?

Something similar happened to Gideon too. Not the reading a book part, but the part about God miraculously affirming that he was a good father. We'll talk more about how God showed himself to be Gideon's father in Part II, but God also used Gideon's human father to bless him.

Jumping ahead in the story slightly, after Gideon spoke to God the first time, God came back to him that night with his first mighty warrior assignment: tear down his dad's pagan altar and burn the fertility statue. Gideon actually did this (!), but he did it in the middle of the night because he was afraid. He clearly feared the men of his town who all did their pagan worship there, but I would bet he was also afraid that his father would disown him if he knew who had done it. When it finally came out that it was Gideon, though, his father rose mightily to the occasion and put himself between Gideon and the angry mob that formed, saying "If Baal really is a god, he can defend himself when someone breaks down his altar" (Judges 6:31). Mic drop. Sarcastic, powerful, and so loving and safe to his son (despite the destruction of his own property)—I love how God works! That kind of confidence and protection is who God our Father is. We can remind ourselves and thank him every day that we walk under it.

God used that moment to turn Gideon's life around. By showing Gideon the love of a good father, God was moving him out of fear and into manhood, teaching him to walk in the trust and love of God, and preparing him for the mighty works ahead of him. Can you believe that God will do the same for you?

PART II

The Lord turned to him and said, "Go in the strength you have and save Israel out of Midian's hand. Am I not sending you?"

Judges 6:14

8. The Lord Turned to Him

Even before He gave Gideon the blessing of his earthly father's defense, God wanted Gideon to know his Divine Father supported him. As we have seen, Gideon greatly doubted this truth and was not afraid to vocalize that doubt. In fact, he ended his first objections to God's call on his life with the accusation that God had abandoned him and his people altogether! Unfazed by this insolence, God's shocking and redemptive response drew Gideon towards becoming the man God meant him to be.

I say God's reply is shocking because it is the exact opposite of what we, in our human logic, would expect. We will look at the redemptive aspects of God's response in the chapters to come, but for now I just want to focus on how unexpectedly wonderful the whole thing is. In my mind, this wonder begins before God even says another word. It starts with a little phrase that's easy to just skip over without thinking about it, one that I had never noticed in all the times I read this story until recently.

The Lord turned to him.

Right after being accused of abandonment and betrayal, God chose to turn toward his accuser instead of away from him. Gideon's words basically amount to an insult of God's character and trustworthiness. If God really had abandoned Israel, he was reneging on many generations' worth of promises like the ones he made to Abraham and Moses. Gideon called God a liar and a traitor (to his face, although without realizing it), and after all that, God turned his face toward Gideon in love.

We don't expect that kind of response from God because we forget that he is not like us. The fathers (and all the other people) we know tend to turn away from us in pain and self-defense when we accuse and disrespect them.

That's what happened to me, anyway. Remember how I said in the last chapter that I had to apologize to my parents for some things? This is part of what I was talking about. Around the time I turned eighteen, I started thinking I was pretty much a full-fledged adult and challenging my father's authority, even though I still lived in his house. To make a long and painful story shorter and... well, maybe just shorter, I was disrespectful and hurtful to him in a variety of ways, to the point that he actually started to retreat from me and my onslaught by withdrawing from our relationship. He probably just wanted to get away from the pain I was causing, and I can't really blame him for trying to defend himself. It's what humans do.

God, however, is not like that. In fact, he is completely unconcerned with his own defense. He takes our best shots like he took Gideon's, without flinching even momentarily from his ongoing plan of turning toward us in love. Now, we can grieve the Lord (which is pretty amazing when you think about it, since he is God and we are pretty much nothing compared to him) like we grieve other people, but unlike how it is with others, God's grief never turns him away from his people. His movement is always towards us, his children, to welcome and restore (see Luke 15:11-32), contrary to Gideon's accusation.

On the other hand, maybe you had a father (or mother—though the Bible mostly uses father imagery, mothers have just as big a role in fostering godly adulthood, especially by encouraging independence and loving us through our failures) who, instead of loving or even retreating, responded to any attack by launching an attack of his own. Maybe when you read that the Lord turned toward Gideon, you can't help thinking that he was just fixing Gideon with an icy stare that made him a target for wrath.

Gideon seemed a bit concerned about that himself after he realized that it was God he had been talking to! God had to specifically reassure him that he wasn't going to be struck dead on the spot. But Gideon could have known God's heart was for him and not against him just from the response God made to his accusations. Not only did God not turn away from Gideon's questions about his character, he also made no move to punish or rebuke Gideon. Instead, he merely reiterated his call of blessing, strength, and guidance on Gideon's life.

God turned toward Gideon when he deserved to be ignored. This is grace. God also refrained from punishing Gideon when he had every right to do so. This is mercy. A gracious and merciful God—is it too good to be true?

Not to tip my hand here, but it isn't. Still, I was living like it was for a long time. I could believe that God would save me from hell and stuff, but I had a lot more trouble understanding how his grace extended to everyday life. When I would mess up, which I'm sure I do about as often as you do, I would always feel like I somehow had to earn my way back to where I was before I slipped. If I slipped again on the way, then I would have to go even further back to feel like I had in some way made up for it. You can probably see how that perspective on life could get to be oppressive rather quickly. It's a recipe for depression.

Recently, though, I've been seeing that just when it seems like God "should" (by my logic) turn away from me until I come back, he actually turns towards me instead. In my darkest moments of sin and despair, when I know I can't save myself, he saves me. When I pick myself up from sliding downhill yet again, I turn around to see that I don't have to climb back up to him because he has already come down to where I am in the middle of my mess to meet me with love.

You know why? Because I'm his son.

That one truth is so important that it's worth reminding yourself about every single day. Every hour, if you need to! Just regularly taking a moment or two to thank God that you are his son or daughter and ask him to help you know and live out all that means is enough to change your life.

My life has been radically changed in the past months by this revelation that God has chosen to welcome me as his son and I can't do anything to stop that. His love for me is absolutely unconditional; that is, no matter how much I might want or try to earn it, I can't. Conversely, I can't earn his rejection either. Or rather, I already have, but he chooses instead to credit to my account the righteousness of Jesus and the Father's love for his only begotten Son. He has given me faith in Jesus, and through that faith he has offered me a permanent adoption into his family. He can do the same for you.

Because of this, I can live without fear. I can take risks, confident in his unchanging love. I can do all the things that a son can do—including growing up.

In fact, I can only be a man because I am his son.

In an unsteady world where it's hard to know what to build on, God's love is the one firm thing I've found. It's the only place I can think of where I would want to try to build manhood. It's a constant in a world of variables: God turns towards me, all the time, every time.

I anticipate a possible objection to the trajectory of my argument here: doesn't God enforce discipline on us? Wouldn't that contradict what I've just said?

To answer, I would say that we also can understand God's discipline only through the lens of sonship. God disciplines only the ones he loves as sons (Proverbs 3:11-12). This is not an attack or a turning against us. God wants us to see even his discipline as part of his love—a movement towards us.

Too often, we confuse discipline with punishment. Punishment says you are guilty of such and such offense, the penalty for which is such and such consequence. No love is involved, just an impartial application of rules. Jesus took the full brunt of this for us on the cross. He became guilty of all our sins and took the punishment for all of them all at once, an unthinkable sacrifice.

There is no leftover punishment for us as God's children. Jesus took *all* of it. As he said, "It is finished."

So what is discipline? The way I see it, discipline is God's way of showing us how something we're doing is killing us until we realize again how much we need him and turn back to him. It's not legal; it's loving! This is exactly what was happening to Israel in our story: they finally saw how their sin with idols had ruined them, and it made them cry out to God—and he sent them Gideon. The goal was not to punish them but to bring them back to relationship with the true God and the blessing that comes with it. The discipline was *better* than the consequences of the road they were walking down without it! God moved towards them, just as he does with us when he convicts us of sin. He doesn't want us to sit around feeling bad; he simply wants us to turn back to him, to draw near to him again.

Think about this: when you love someone, you want them to know it. So when you tell them, you turn to face them and look them right in the eyes. Discipline is one way God does this, just like his constant acceptance of us despite our doubts and accusations is another. In both cases, he fixes his eyes directly on us to prove the truth of his love.

Even when we deserve to be turned away from, God turns toward us every time. What could our lives start to look like as we apprehend this truth?

9. Go

I'm still pretty new at this, but one thing I've noticed about my life since I've begun to understand more about God's constant love toward me is that it has more *movement* than it did before. As love drives out fear, it sets us free to do more things! They don't have to turn out exactly right, either. Even if (and when) they don't, we can glorify God just by resting in his love as we take the risks inherent in manhood.

This pattern seems to be the one God was setting before Gideon. After he told Gideon who he was and that he was with him, the next word out of God's mouth was simply "Go." Although Gideon was busy missing the point at the time, this instruction made perfect sense to God—I'm with you, and I made you to be mighty, so go ahead and just do it!

Without doing too much borrowing of a certain shoe company's trademarked phrase so as to avoid any controversy or legal action, let me just say here that I think there's a reason certain company catchphrases actually catch on. Nike's slogan resonates with people for reasons I bet they don't even understand! They've inadvertently hit on something that's at the very core of our designed identity as men and women of God. If God is with us, we don't need to shrink back wondering if life will work out. We just have to get up and do it. The freedom and strength of this lifestyle calls out to the deep places of our souls.

It's very important to remember, though, that shoe advertising has only grasped half the truth—and it's the second half. The first part, without which the second is meaningless, is that God has to be with us. If he isn't, then "just doing it" is nothing more than a frightening succession of trials and errors with potentially devastating consequences. That's why so many people *wish* they could just do life, but still find themselves paralyzed by fear, doubt, and insecurity—just like Gideon. Life can be scary, and without the Lord I'm surprised that anyone finds the courage to attempt it at all. Maybe that's how we get stuck trying desperately to achieve our own safety and pleasure instead of doing anything risky.

God has to be with us, or the command to go will seem like a death sentence. As Moses prayed, God, if you're not coming too, don't send us! Whether God tells you to go defeat a whole army and save a nation or just to become a man who does his will whatever the cost, it will seem so impossible that it would surely end in your death if you don't believe he's with you.

Unfortunately, just reading the truth that God *is* with you if you trust in Jesus probably won't be enough to convince you. You don't need *me* to tell you; you need God to tell you. Truth is always truth, but until he actually reveals it to our hearts, we have a shocking ability to just not get it. So ask him. Get in God's face, and ask him who he made you to be. Ask him to show you that he's with you and that he loves you. Give your life to him and ask what he wants to do with it. He will tell you.

It might take time, but it's vital not to skip this step. And it's not a one-time deal, either. I'm trying to keep on doing this over and over, like refueling my tanks of faith in God's love and plan. Knowing that God loved me and was with me yesterday won't do it for me. I need to know it today, and if that takes spending more time with him first, then I do that. The results so far have been wonderful—not in the sense of arrival, but in peace on the journey.

Even when you know that God is with you, though, there are a few ways I've managed to find for this whole "Go" thing to go wrong. The first one works like this. You realize that God being with you should free you up to move and run, which is true. Then, you realize that your church is involved in a whole bunch of really great ministries, which is wonderful. Next, you start finding out that every single one of those ministries is looking for young, energetic believers to help them carry out the vision God has given them—not that there's anything wrong with that. The problem begins when you let the approval of leaders and the praise you get for participating become your motivating force instead of your knowledge that God is with you and loves you.

That's what I did. When I finally ended up in a church that was actually doing the things the Bible says to do, I wanted to do all of it right away. I think this came from a good place in my heart—years of teaching finally clicking into place with action and a desire to please God. Unfortunately, also in my heart was a desperate desire for human approval and praise, both of which you will certainly get if you start doing a whole bunch of ministry all at once. Once that praise and its associated feelings of worth started kicking in, I got lost.

Before I knew it, I was somehow involved in almost every ministry our church was offering. Meanwhile, my personal relationship with God, the life-breath of knowing his presence and love, was being suffocated. I got so caught up in doing things *for* God (as if he needs that anyway!) that I lost track of just being *with* him. All the things I was doing were good things—kingdom works, even. And they were killing me.

The thing is, living this way looks so good to most people who don't see deeply into your heart that it's very hard (especially if you're good at hiding/ignoring what's really going on in your heart, like I am) to find anyone who will tell you not to do this. So let me be that person. Don't do this! Even if you don't think it's possible now, you'll burn yourself out, because approval and the praise of men are false gods. Like all other false gods, all they can do is consume. They take and take and never give and always keep you wanting more, even when you have no energy left to go after them any longer. Then after you burn out chasing idols, you'll likely blame God because he's the one who started it all by loving you and telling you to move. Because you're blaming him, you won't draw near to him, which is the only place you can possibly go to rest and be healed. So the cycle continues. At least, that's how it went for me. That kind of movement was not the manhood I was looking for. It felt aimless and desperate, not strong.

It also led right into me learning about another way we can mishandle God's instruction to Go. Once I had the "Aha!" moment that I was spreading myself like butter over too much bread (to use the hobbitish phrase), I decided to solve the problem by stopping everything and getting my act together behind the scenes before I would do anything else. That makes such good logical sense that it's hard to see why it was a bad idea, but it was. The problem is subtle, but essentially it's that if I'll only act once I fully have my life in order, I'll never act! And that's pretty much what happened with me. Thankfully, I love music and worship so much that I didn't give up worship ministry, so I was still doing something, which God eventually used to help bring me back to health. Anyway, I *did* need to stop doing a lot of things, but feeling all put together wasn't the answer to the problem. The real answer was coming back to resting in God's love.

I should note here that God has a lot of grace for this mistake I was making. He certainly had grace for Gideon wanting to be exactly sure of things before he moved (see Judges 6:36-40). In fact, if it comes down to a choice between busily doing everything and dropping it all to sit at the feet of the Lord, God is pretty clear on which one we should choose—just ask Mary and Martha (Luke 10:38-42). God does call us to seasons of rest where we simply spend time with him. As I've said several times already, it is vital that we are willing to be with him in stillness.

We need to be still. God, though, is not a stationary God. He goes places, and he does things. In order to continue to be with him, we have to recognize when he's on the move. Of course, he never leaves us behind in the sense of forsaking us, but we can miss out on opportunities if we are only willing to spend time with him in stillness, not in action. The trick is learning not to get ahead of him or fall behind him on the action part. It's easy to get antsy and move too fast, especially with the pressure of becoming a man. It's also easy to move too slowly out of fear.

So, two ways we can respond wrongly when God says "Go" are to get caught up in frantically doing things *for* him, and to try just to be *with* him without being willing to do anything.

God invites us into adulthood by asking us to *do* things *with* him.

Of course, sometimes those things will be resting, being still, and just talking. Other times, he wants us to move as parts of the plans he enacts in the world. We can't make either one into a hard and fast rule. In fact, knowing God is not about rules at all, but relationship. It's about doing whatever God is doing, not because we have to but because all we want is to be with him, because he loves us with such a powerful, compelling and peaceful love.

To do something *with* God rather than *for* him is to recognize that he doesn't need our help. He is fully capable of getting his plans accomplished by any number of other means. However, he has chosen to use us as his instruments and given us the privilege of participating in his work. He has even planned good things for each of us to walk in based on how he uniquely made us with different gifts and abilities (Ephesians 2:10). We don't even have to make this stuff happen—his plans are already in motion all over the world, just waiting for us to step right into them.

In Gideon's place and time, God's plan was saving his whole nation from enemy occupation. This leads right into a final way we can Go wrong.

Part of my becoming a man has to be finding out what part of God's plan he wants me to step into in each season. I don't know what it is completely even in this season, much less the rest of my life, but I'm keeping my eyes open. I think writing this book is part of it. I'm learning so much, and the more I learn about God and his love, the more possibilities open up. Problem is, the whole thing is so big that it can feel pretty overwhelming. I have the desire to see God do so many things that I don't have the first clue how to accomplish.

I can't help thinking Gideon probably felt the same way. Save a whole nation? Just one dude? How would you have felt if God told you to do that? Where would you begin?

That last question is the key one. We can also go wrong in obeying God's command to "Go" if we feel like we have to accomplish his whole plan all at once. It's impossible, and trying to do it can only lead to paralysis. Attempting the whole thing at once pretty much only guarantees that we'll never start! All God is asking us to do is remember that saving the nation (or whatever plan he asks us to work on) is *his* plan that he's already doing, and we are simply participating because that's how we can be with him. We just have to start in the faith that he will lead us as we go, and before we know it we'll be knee-deep in his plan.

We just have to do the next right thing. Not all the right things at once, not even two of them at once, just the next one. That's a bit more manageable, no?

Maybe Gideon, like us, was paralyzed by the enormity of the plan God was laying out before him. By the night after God told him to just "Go," he still hadn't gone anywhere or done anything! But God is so good. Instead of judging him, God came back and told him what the next right thing for him to do was! I bet Gideon had no idea how tearing apart his father's idol-worshipping station was connected to saving Israel from their enemies. But he didn't need to know that; the important thing was that he just did it. Then, God used that one action, that one right thing, to make him into something of a popular hero, a bold man people could follow as a leader in war.

What I take from that episode is that God can tell us what the next right thing is too. He might not give us the whole plan. He might, I suppose, but that wasn't what happened to Gideon at all: God kept giving him instructions one step at a time the whole way, as we'll see. There was no "Here's the plan with a list of steps; now do it, see you later." It was all about relationship and fellowship all the time: "Here's what I'm doing next, and here's how you can be part of it."

It's not like the next right thing will always be super-counterintuitive or hard to discover, either. To take perhaps the most practical example possible, say God wants me to write a book. I could easily sit around thinking, "How do I write a book? How do I publish a book? What else do I need to know?" Or, I could just write the next page. Better yet, I could spend time with the Lord asking him to lead me and then write it.

God wants me to be so secure in his love that I'll go wherever he goes and do whatever he does knowing that I am always his son. I don't have to do everything all at once, or even one big thing all at once, or feel like I have my act completely together. In stillness or in motion, God has a plan for me to join in, and he invites me to become a man as I discover it one step at a time. All I have to do is Go.

Like Gideon, I still question my own ability at times. But I know I can just go, and so can you. What plans could we find ourselves walking into as we do?

10. The Strength You Have

Like Gideon, I already know some of what God has to say about me. Also like him, I tend to disregard God's word and tell God all the things I'm not. Gideon simply was not aware of the strength he had, and that's pretty much the same problem many aspiring men have today. Everyone is telling us to be strong, but it feels like trying to draw water from an empty well. Is there really anything down there to draw up if it comes down to it?

Here's a quick summary of what we know about Gideon so far: God called him a mighty warrior, and he ignored God and questioned God's love with complaints about Israel's current situation.

Now it was God's turn to ignore Gideon. Notice how God continues undeterred with the same theme after Gideon's objections. It was "mighty warrior" before the objections, so after them he picks right up and says "Go in the strength you have" (Judges 6:14). Essentially he's saying: "I just told you that you have strength, so go use it."

Gideon obviously had no idea what that strength was. Seeing that God had no interest in defending himself against the charge of abandonment, Gideon was forced to go back down the ladder of doubt to his doubt of himself. He came up with a well-reasoned case based on his lowly personal and family situation to argue that he didn't have any strength to draw from, and he challenged God to refute him.

God made no attempt to do so.

He didn't contradict any of Gideon's statements about who he was. Instead, he said, "I will be with you, and you will strike down [literally: smite, which I like better] all the Midianites together" (Judges 6:16). God was so matter of fact—like it was a foregone conclusion.

This was obviously a clue to what God had meant when he mentioned the strength Gideon had, but it meant nothing to Gideon at the time. Think how you would feel if a stranger came up to you and said you'd be fine in a huge impending battle simply because he would be there! Yeah, thanks bro, that makes me feel a lot better. In order for Gideon to make any sense out of the strength God was offering, God would have to reveal himself to Gideon.

That's exactly what he began to do. Clearly, God's supremely confident assertion got Gideon thinking about what kind of person could make such a claim. He decided he'd better offer this important person a meal, at least. When said meal exploded into flame and was consumed before him, perhaps Gideon got his first glimpse of the strength God had been referring to.

Unfortunately, he was too busy being scared for his life at the time to notice, but God used even that to reveal his own character to Gideon. Rather than striking Gideon dead for his insolence, God offered him a blessing. So he was strong, but also merciful and kind. Maybe this *was* the kind of God who would use Gideon to save his people! If Gideon had him on his side, then maybe there was a chance.

The blessing God gave Gideon is important too: he gave him peace. This is *shalom* in Hebrew, and it means more than just serenity, the normal English sense of the word peace. Shalom also signifies wholeness and completion. God showed that he himself *is* peace, and Gideon recognized it (Judges 6:24). With God's power, Gideon could be complete, fully confident and equipped for even the most daunting task.

So, here's a quick summary of what we know about *me* so far: I long to become a strong, godly man, and I already know from God's Word that I am called to do so, but I doubt myself because I doubt God's love and so I come to him with questions about whether he is even with me at all.

Can you guess what his response has been?

He doesn't defend himself to me; he has too much confidence for that. Instead, he says Go in the strength you have and become a man.

When I counter with my lists of reasons why I'm not strong enough to do that, he doesn't argue with me there either. He knows it's true. But then he says "I will be with you" and changes the whole equation. And he doesn't just say it to me, but to any who will follow him and believe in his death-conquering, enemy-smiting, manhood-making strength (see Matthew 28:20, Hebrews 13:5, et al.). Actually, he hasn't said anything to me about doing any smiting yet—his plan for saving people is much less martial these days (But lest you fear missing out, check out Revelation 19 as well!).

Anyway, much like he did for Gideon, God has chosen to reveal himself to us so that we know what kind of power we have on our side. He can and does do this both through personal revelation and through the promises in the Bible. What if we lived like they were really true? What if I really have become a new creation in Christ, been adopted as the King's son, been given the armor of God to wear, and received all the other promises of the New Testament?

What if there really is "no condemnation for those who are in Christ Jesus" (Romans 8:1)?

The reasons I bring to God that I think make me unfit for the task of being a godly man usually have to do with all the ways I've managed to mess up in life. I come to him telling him what a sinner I am and how I can't even seem to avoid sinning consistently, much less show his love to others.

Maybe you identify. "God, why am I always so selfish?" "God, it's been three weeks since I even read the Bible..." "God, I can't believe I was on those sites again—am I even a Christian?" Let's be real here.

What we expect God to say in response is something like "Yeah, better clean that up and fix yourself before you take on this crazy plan I have."

What he actually says is "I am with you."

There is no condemnation.

You are my child, because *all* your sin was completely and eternally covered by my Son.

I (not you) make you complete.

This is reality, and only in the true and total embrace of reality do we find freedom. The unimaginable truth is that, by the Holy Spirit, Jehovah Shalom has cleaned us, redeemed us, and made his home inside our souls. In him we have peace and are made complete to do what God calls us to do. Just like it was for Gideon, this is the strength we have, the strength we are supposed to go in.

This takes time to realize. That's why, despite the whole chapter about just going, it's been months between when I wrote that and when I'm writing this! Maybe I wasn't ready; these things are just starting to become real to me. But the wholeness and peace I'm beginning to experience as they do become my reality can only be explained by a God who IS wholeness and peace. I'm *going* now—which brings me to another important thing to remember.

Even once he knew that it was God himself asking him to go save the nation, Gideon probably wasn't *feeling* completely at ease with what he was supposed to do—and that's ok. Sometimes what we feel is not the same as what is true. What's important is that the knowledge got Gideon to start *doing* what he was supposed to do, which led to God showing him whole new levels of his power (which then made him feel better too!).

In fact, once he started down this track of faith, the Bible says that the Holy Spirit (the same one Jesus sent to us—see Acts 1:7-8) came upon—more literally, covered or clothed—Gideon and suddenly gave him the strength to muster a huge army. God hadn't even mentioned to him that this could happen. God actually asked him to go in this strength before he had it and then gave it to him on the way!

But we already have the Holy Spirit, if we believe in Jesus. Have you ever heard Christians talk about how God can do more than we imagine? That's easy to handle if it's some vague power of a God outside us, but what the whole verse says is that God is "able to do immeasurably more than all we ask or imagine, according to his power that is at work *within us*" (Ephesians 3:20, emphasis added). God's plan for using his unimaginable power is to do it through us! We just might not start to see it until we obey and get out beyond what our own flimsy strength can handle. Along with all the promises, we've already been given this incredible extra strength to go in as we become the men and women God is calling us to be. What can we accomplish walking in that strength?

11. Save Israel

Could I and people like me in my generation be the ones to bring a nation back to God?

I'm starting to realize that this whole growing up thing is about a lot more than just me becoming a man. I mean, I know God wants all of us to grow more fully into the people he's made us to be. It just seems like that's nowhere near big enough to be God's end goal. What if this is just a step on the way to something much bigger? And what if God wants me to know that scary yet exhilarating truth to get me moving?

The God I see in the Bible is not a God of almost enough or just barely sufficient. He is the God of abundance, of more than we ask or imagine, of enough and some left over. He could have fed the five thousand people (John 6:1-13) with exactly enough miraculously multiplied food, but instead he did it with twelve baskets of leftovers! He could've just given

Abraham a son; instead, he gave him a whole nation of descendants. There are countless more examples in Scripture and history—there is always more with God.

God also didn't stop with convincing Gideon he was a mighty warrior. In fact, he turned one of Gideon's own objections to the whole deal into his mission in life: Oh, so you say I must not be with you because Midian is beating you into the dust? Funny you should mention that, because the reason I actually just came here was to call you, mighty warrior, to go and save Israel from Midian!

Okay, maybe God is not as sarcastic-sounding as I am. Still, he didn't come to the winepress only to affirm Gideon's manhood. God definitely wanted to bless Gideon personally by launching him out of cowardice into courage and helping him be a man. But God also wanted Gideon to know who he was as a child of the Almighty so that he could take his place in the things God had already been planning.

God didn't just give Gideon manhood. He gave him a mission.

Or maybe you could say that the two are one and the same. God saw the truth of who Gideon was because he had made Gideon a mighty warrior, but for Gideon to take hold of that calling and become the man God made him to be, he had to actually do what warriors do and save his people. The manhood and the mission were inseparably linked.

It's the same way today. God is giving me a mission to go with my manhood.

It's the same mission he gave Gideon.

Does that sound crazy? It might if you think I'm talking about military conquest! But that's not what this is about at all. I mean, the deliverance of Israel wasn't the end goal of what God told Gideon to do, either. Let me explain.

I realize, of course, that my nation is not under the oppressive control of a hostile enemy. Well, actually, we have pretty much been invaded and occupied by the ubiquitous, self-focused media machine. Unfortunately, the nation I'm talking about here could just as easily be America as it could be the Church, but it's the church that I want to focus on. America will never be saved without the church being saved anyway! In any case, our salvation won't come through military violence. Our battle is not even against people (Ephesians 6:12), but against the evil powers of this age (for example, media-sanctioned self-centeredness and avarice, addiction, human trafficking and racism, just to name a few—more on this in part 4). Clearly, the mighty warriors of today are called to fight differently.

The real question I'm asking is *why* God told Gideon to go and save Israel. The methods may change with time, but God's larger purpose is still the same.

Israel was God's chosen nation. They were the people he specifically set apart from the rest to worship him and spread his blessings to the rest of humanity. God repeatedly affirmed this calling through promises to their patriarchs, men like Abraham and Moses (see Genesis 12:1-3 and Exodus 19:3-6, among many other passages on this theme). They were supposed to be a kingdom of priests, worshiping God and drawing others to do the same.

Sadly, they kept on failing to fulfill God's calling. They tended to stop worshiping God when things went well, which also caused them to cease being his representatives to the rest of the world. When that happened, God would send their enemies to oppress them until they remembered that God was their strength and cried out to him. Then God would graciously save them and cause his name to be glorified among the nations again—until they fell back into sin.

The Old Testament records the way this cycle repeated itself many times, and Gideon found himself in the midst of one of the first ones. God told him to save Israel not just because he needed to be a man or because his nation needed him (although those were also true), but even more because God wanted to set apart a people who would worship him.

God never changes. This is what he still wants today.

In the New Testament, we see how we, as the followers of Jesus in his Church (with a capital C) around the world, have also had the calling of being God's chosen worshippers opened to us. Now we are the royal priesthood, the nation God has set apart to praise him (1 Peter 2:9-10).

However, the church, just like Israel did, has a tendency toward failure in this calling. We fail either by becoming so much like the world that we no longer inspire it to the higher call of worshiping the Lord of everything, or by becoming so self-centered and small-minded (i.e. afraid) that we break the body of Christ into exclusive little fragments that abandon the greater mission and try to operate on their own.

One way joins the Midianites; the other climbs down into the winepress.

Does it start to make sense how the mission of godly manhood and womanhood is the same today as it was for Gideon? Manhood is and has always been about much more than mere self-actualization. It must be. Just as much if not more than ever, God is calling for a people to rise up and restore his name to a position of honor and glory. He wants us to be men because he wants to be worshiped.

I know this is what God is calling me to do. More than finding a job or a wife or making my own way in the world, he wants me to become a man who will worship him in every single thing I do, say or think (Colossians 3:17). But it's not just about me. If that was the end, Gideon could have just stopped after he offered the sacrifice God commanded. Instead, God called him to save Israel.

What if the church, the new Israel, needs to be saved? What if it needs to be gathered out of the enemy camp and out of the shattered disunity in which it finds itself so that it can learn to worship God again? Who will make this happen?

I believe it will only happen through a generation of men and women being born into true spiritual adulthood. The church needs a generation who will devote themselves to praising God and seeing his name lifted high, finding out along the way just how mighty they are in him. It is not about us, but about joining God's ongoing mission of setting apart a people to worship him.

Gideon's mission and mine are the same. Become a man, and fight to save God's people from the powers of evil that stand against them so that, above all else, the Lord will receive the glory he is fully due, both in the church and from those who haven't yet seen any reason to join.

Does that sound too big? I know I've often felt unworthy to do anything really big or significant for God, both because of my own weakness and because I don't have any sort of high standing according to the world. (Those sound an awful lot like the same objections Gideon had, by the way.) What I'm beginning to take hold of, though, is that I *am* worthy of whatever calling God places on me, simply because he says so.

There is no higher authority to appeal to. Save a nation? Save his Church? Inspire people to worship him? I can do all of that, but only if he qualifies me to do it. The only strength I have to go in is him.

That's why when I say my mission is the same as Gideon's, I don't mean to make myself somehow special, like I'm the only one. If it were just for me, there would be no reason to write this book. His mission is yours too. Gideon had an army (albeit a smaller one than he wanted) with him to fulfill God's mission, and it will take a whole generation of worshipers to bring the church back (or forward) to the unity and purity God desires. I'm willing to lead the charge if that's what God wants, but honestly I'd be just as happy somewhere in the middle of the army if we were really charging ahead.

Isn't that what you want too? To be part of something bigger than yourself, bigger than finding your own way? Becoming a man of God is always about the larger purpose of bringing glory and honor to God's name alongside the people he has chosen.

The second half of this book is about how Gideon did just that.

We can too. Do you believe it?

12. Am I Not Sending You?

If you don't believe you can fulfill God's mission for you, why not put him to the test? That's what Gideon did!

Well, to answer my own question, there are actually some pretty good reasons not to. Better stated, there's one really good reason, which is also why Gideon thought for sure he was going to die after he found out he'd been talking to God the whole time he was angrily voicing his doubts. This was not just him being a scaredy-cat; he knew his history.

In the Bible, testing God usually results in death.

Death. Usually instantaneous, sometimes just your own, sometimes yours plus your whole family's, sometimes more painful than other times, but still death. Seriously, this happens a *bunch* of times in the Old Testament, and even at least once in the New. God sent poisonous snakes, brought plagues, spontaneously combusted people, opened the ground under them, had them killed by others, or struck people dead on the spot, among other methods. The common thread in all these circumstances? They put God to the test.

So the question is: why did Gideon get away with it?

The Bible is pretty clear on the point that testing God is a bad idea. Deuteronomy 6:16 summarizes the Israelites' experiences in that area in a handy, easy to remember rule: "Do not put the Lord your God to the test." Simple. Also, it was important enough that Jesus quoted it to Satan when he was being tempted, and the apostle Paul also said something very similar (Matthew 4:7 and 1 Corinthians 10:9, respectively). It's a recurring theme.

But then the Bible also says another thing. One single time in the whole huge book, tucked away right at the end of the Old Testament in the little book of Malachi (3:10), God challenges his people to test him. God puts himself on the line and says he will bless Israel if they will bring him all the offerings he had asked for—and with a much more abundant blessing than they would ever experience if they tried to hold onto their wealth themselves. Basically, God said here's the truth, now act like it's true and see what happens.

Why is that important? It means that testing God is not necessarily an across-the-board death sentence. It's a good thing, too, or there would probably be a lot more dead people.

Anyway, there may be specific ways to test God that he tolerates or even approves of. Maybe it's more about the heart of the tester and his or her relationship with God than about a specific rule. God's concern for the heart over mere outward obedience is another running theme in Scripture.

So the question *really* is: What made Gideon's tests different from all the ones that got people killed?

I say tests, because Gideon didn't test God just that one time with the whole meal offering. Later on, he launched two even more audacious tests, for a grand total of three times that he *didn't* get struck dead. There's no way he could have gotten lucky three times. The difference had to be in his heart before God. The story gives us some clues about where Gideon's heart was that help explain the whole thing. Just clues, mind you—not proof. But consider what I have to say and see if it lines up with what you know about God.

God had said to Gideon as his final guarantee of success, "Am I not sending you?" (Judges 6:14). Gideon would have understood that to be sent by someone means to go in *all* of that person's authority and power, just like God had sent Moses to Pharaoh in Egypt long before. What Gideon did not know, however, was anything about the person who was sending him! Clearly God had never spoken like this to Gideon before, and he had no idea what was going on. So rather than expecting him to know something he could not yet understand, God gave Gideon a chance to get to know who he was.

As we discussed in chapter 10, God showed Gideon a glimpse of his power and his mercy in the first test, when Gideon brought him an offering to see what he would do with it. Now Gideon knew something explosive about what it meant to be sent by the Lord in all his power, and even more importantly this sparked Gideon's personal *relationship* with his God.

This is consistent with the way God later used the prophet Malachi to challenge Israel to put him to the test. God wanted to reveal something to them about what it meant to follow him. He told them the truth about who he was, then told them to act like it was true and see if he didn't back it up. It was about God's people learning to live in relationship with him.

This is also very consistent with my experience of God as a young believer. As an example, when I was in high school I had a friend from a different school who was having a lot of trouble with another girl there. She and this other girl were apparently at odds due to both liking the same boy in their class—perhaps you remember how high school drama goes. Anyway, things were starting to get nasty, and my friend was desperate when she asked me what to do. I was just starting to walk in faith in God at the time, so I told her that she should pray for this other girl at home, and then again anytime it looked like they might start fighting. After she left I realized the potential firestorm I might have just sent her into, and then *I* prayed, telling God he had better back me up and not let her get eaten alive!

Well, my friend (bless her heart) actually believed what I said more than I did, and she tried what I suggested. The very next day at school, the girl who had been giving her such a hard time came up to her and, as my friend braced herself and began nervously praying, started apologizing for everything! They both burst into tears (so I'm told) as high school girls tend to do, had a heart-to-heart talk, and became fast friends that day. They still are. In fact, years later, that other girl and her husband (not the same guy they were fighting over) are now good friends of mine too!

God had something to teach me in that situation about who he is. He doesn't always resolve things that quickly and painlessly, of course, but rather than being angry with me, he wanted me to know as a young Christian that he really would back me up if I would believe and act like he is who he said he is. I became a little more of a man that day because of it.

He told me the truth, challenged me to act on it, and then backed up my test of him. That's just what he did for Israel through Malachi. It's also what he did for Gideon.

Once God showed his true character of power and mercy to Gideon by accepting his offering, Gideon understood what it meant that this God was sending him. He started acting like it was true and becoming a man of God, doing crazy and powerful things in the strength he had (which was God!). God never stopped backing him up. In fact, the new faith Gideon experienced after testing God the first time lasted him through causing an uproar in his family and city by tearing down their pagan altar, almost getting killed by the townsfolk but instead becoming a folk hero for his bravery, and then using his newfound status to blow the trumpets of war and gather an army some 32,000 strong to go and save Israel!

But then his faith wavered.

There he found himself, with an army massing behind him, questioning whether what he had set out to do was really possible. Maybe things were taking a while to take shape and that gave him time to doubt. It's also possible that he delayed the whole operation two days for no other reason than to ask God to prove himself by doing things that were naturally impossible (Judges 6:36-40). What made these later tests acceptable to God?

Actually, God never said they were (or weren't) acceptable. He just did the impossible things Gideon asked for. I'm assuming that means he wasn't offended, but he chose to remain silent. When God didn't say anything to the challenge, I'm sure Gideon thought God was gone and he was a goner. But then Gideon's audacious requests were matter-of-factly granted. Why?

On the face of it, this situation reminds me a lot of the way Gideon's ancestors tested God in the wilderness. After God miraculously brought them out of bondage in Egypt, they made it partway across the desert, got thirsty and started testing the Lord. They complained, claiming that he had brought them out to kill them, that it would have been better if they had stayed, that they had nothing to eat/drink/look at, and so on. There are at least five episodes like that in Exodus through Deuteronomy, and they all end with casualties. These people were rebellious, and they made God mad.

Gideon was also partway into a long and dangerous mission and doubting God enough that he wouldn't move forward. The only thing I can think of that he did differently is in the way he approached God. He wasn't arrogant, he didn't complain and he affirmed that God had indeed already promised to do what Gideon now didn't quite believe he would.

Gideon wasn't rebellious. He was just afraid.

He wasn't questioning God's plan; I think he knew full well what God wanted him to do but was scared to do it. Having experienced the power God demonstrated in receiving his offering, now he would need to experience the mercy. He did. God came to him in grace and reassured his honest and fearful heart by accepting his tests.

God knows that our keenest resolve can quickly grow dull. I was asking God for direction in my life the other day, pleading with him to show me the next step I should take. Instead, what I felt him speak to my spirit was, "Are you doing the things I've already told you to do?" Well no, I wasn't. I got tired of those things and was hoping he would give me new ones! It was a convicting moment. But he didn't strike me dead. God knows that I lose focus, and he has always been gracious to point me back in the right direction as many times as I need it when I come to him in honesty. His response cut through my fear and put me back on the right path.

Gideon lost his focus too, but he didn't lose the heart to serve God. He was probably just as scared as any soldier would be before his first battle, but even more so because he would be leading the charge. Also, God hadn't promised him he would survive—only that the Israelites would win! He was afraid, but he still desperately longed to succeed in doing what God had asked—at least if he was anything like I am.

In fact, he was so afraid (as you probably have experienced, fear doesn't always make sense) that he did something even more dangerous than going to battle: he tested the God of the world. This God, though—not only did he show mercy, but he showed that he knew Gideon's heart and affirmed their growing relationship by coming through for him. God would challenge him again soon enough. For the time being, his silent fulfillment of Gideon's requests echoed his earlier question with all that it had meant.

It's the same question God is asking us as he makes us into men today: Am I not sending you?

PART III

The Lord said to Gideon, "You have too many men for me to deliver Midian into their hands. In order that Israel may not boast against me that her own strength has saved her, announce now to the people, 'Anyone who trembles with fear may turn back…'"

Judges 7:2-3

13. Too Many Men

Knowing that he was sent in the power and blessing of God, Gideon was finally starting to believe the Lord would really do what he said he would. He had helped Gideon gather a sizable army and had even allowed him to work through his fear by testing God.

Now it was God's turn to test Gideon.

Of course, God feels no need to get the best of his people or get back at them for things. He actually gave his own completely different reasons for what he was about to do to Gideon, so it's not like the tests were payback. But just as Gideon had tested God twice, God put Gideon to the test twice by decimating his army. Actually, decimating is putting it too lightly (even though the people removed weren't killed) because decimation originally referred to an army being cut by one-tenth. God cut Gideon's army by 9.9-tenths.

God told Gideon that his army of approximately 32,000 (which still would have been vastly outnumbered, by the way) was too many men and reduced it first to 10,000 (still too many) and then to a tiny band of just 300! For those of you who think English majors can't do math, that's less than one percent of the original force. If you compare that number to the total given later for the armies they were fighting, you find out that God sent Gideon into battle outnumbered about 450 to 1.

That doesn't make sense.

Yes, God had given a reason for it, and we can explain it theologically. But militarily? It's ludicrous. Gideon was already scared when he had 32,000; I'm sure he vehemently disagreed that it was too many! But then again, Gideon had already asked God for two things that made no sense either, and God did both of those things. I can't help but think that part of why God responded to Gideon's tests the way he did and then directly followed that with his own incomprehensible plan for victory was to teach Gideon something about the way he does things.

God doesn't always make sense.

I'm not saying God is illogical. He created logic and gave it to us as a gift. However, our capacity to reason logically has been marred by sin, along with every other aspect of our personhood. Even if it hadn't been, we are still God's creations, and his ways are simply higher than ours—by an immeasurable distance and across the board, like the sky is always higher than the earth (Isaiah 55:9). If we fully understood God, then that would mean we would be God, not him! Right?

That, by the way, is the oldest temptation known to man. Become like God, understand what he's doing—the same carrot (or apple?) on the same stick that Satan tricked Adam and Eve with. He planted the same worthless question in their minds that he does in ours (as discussed in chapter 5): *why* did God _____ (do this, say that, ask us to do something, etc.)? Ever since that moment, humanity has been trying to figure God out instead of knowing and trusting him.

Yet throughout Scripture, we see a God who does things we can't explain. Let me give just two examples out of many.

God asked Abraham to take his only son, the same son God had already promised to make a great nation out of, and kill him as a sacrifice. Ever since I was a kid, this story has bothered me. Seriously, it's right there in the Ten Commandments: don't kill people. God told Abraham to break his own law. Sure, you could argue that the law hadn't been given yet, but God had put a curse on someone for killing someone else already. Yes, whoever wrote Hebrews tells us Abraham reasoned that God could raise Isaac from the dead, but God had asked for a *burnt offering*. There wasn't going to be any Isaac left to raise. In fact, this story finally got written down about the same time as the laws about burnt offerings being completely consumed, as well as the law against murder it seems to ignore. It had to have messed with people then too, like it has with me. Maybe that's why God put it in his book. Even with God's explanation to Abraham that it was a test of faith, it doesn't make sense. God knows everything; he doesn't *need* to test people!

God is hard enough to understand when he explains himself, but sometimes he doesn't even do that—just ask Job. As I mentioned in chapter 5, God let Satan tear Job's life apart, and then God put it back together even better than it was before. But he didn't explain any of it. Job asked him to justify himself over and over, but all God said was essentially "I am God, you are not, and I don't have to explain myself to you." No predictable moral, like "I had to break you down to build you up" or "good things come to those who wait." Just Job left speechless before the God who took the time to talk to him. It's a thoroughly shocking story; nothing in it is what you would expect. Still, God gave it a pretty sizable chunk of space in the one book he has specifically given us to help us get to know him.

That's exactly the point: knowing him. After all, God didn't ask us to be still and understand that he is God. He wants us to *know* (Psalm 46:10). There's certainly a difference. I doubt my future wife will care too much if I always understand everything about her. I think she'll want me to know her—in the sense of who she is and what she cares about and what makes her, well, *her* (And hopefully in the KJV sense too, but that's a totally different issue, as well as a fascinating linguistic choice). Anyway, it could be that part of why God is teaching me this now is so that I don't mess up my marriage someday.

But again, it's not about why. See how deeply ingrained this desire to make sense out of everything is?

Somehow, I always thought that as I became a man life would just start to make more sense. I mean, the people I see and talk to always seem to have their lives so figured out and put together! The people who I really know well, though, are open enough with me to admit they don't have it all figured out. The ones I really respect are okay with it too. That's comforting to me because it lines up with my observation that life has certainly **not** started making more sense as I get older. God still hasn't shown me the reasons for most of the world's problems or even my own. Maybe manhood is not about knowing more of the answers but about asking better questions.

Actually, it might be a relief to stop trying to figure things out! It's a lot of work trying to find the reasons for everything and understand all the craziness of life. God is offering to handle that burden for us. He offers us the much more restful option of just getting to know him in all of it. It's not quite the same as getting to know a human person, though. Another reason God sometimes seems not to make sense is that, even though he never changes, he's so big that there's always something new to learn about him.

So, what if God wants me to do something that doesn't make sense to me? How can I do that unless I know him and trust that he is good even if I don't see it? And how can I get that knowledge and trust unless he gives it to me?

I guess the question is, what if the manhood God wants for me is something so dangerous and counter-intuitive that anyone looking on would say it was foolishness? Like, say, facing an army of 135,000 with 300 guys? Because that didn't make any sense. But Gideon tried it because he knew the One who was sending him, and, even crazier, it ended up being the perfect plan.

God allowed Gideon to get to know him through talking with him and even through the tests, and *then* God asked him to do something unbelievable, and it worked. That's how Gideon became a man, but perhaps it didn't happen in accomplishing the mission so much as it did in knowing and believing God enough to accept the task even though it was a logical impossibility.

Could God be giving me a task that big, that important—that impossible? Like changing the culture of a dying city, or inspiring a new generation to worship him in spirit and truth? It scares me, but I feel like he is. Maybe you feel the same. Can we be a generation of spiritual maturity forged by saying yes to the impossible, impractical, illogical mission of God? I believe we can. But it won't happen until we see the mission, however crazy it might be, as just one aspect of knowing the incredible God who sends us—and helping others know him as well.

Will I be content to follow a God who doesn't always make sense or explain himself to me? Can I just be still and know him?

We become men and women of God not by figuring out the world but by personally getting to know its Creator. So, what does he want us to know?

14. That Israel May Not Boast

God is big enough to speak to all of us and relate to us individually, and he chooses to reveal himself in many different ways to different people. The whole Bible is full of these stories—it seems like God never does things the same way twice! Yet this is the record we have been given of who he is. What are we supposed to take from these stories? Should we wait for a holy messenger to light our dinner on fire before we talk to God? Do we keep putting fleece on the ground until something happens?

I wouldn't suggest it. However, I still think the stories are important, and this is why: although God's methods of revealing himself are as varied and unique as the people he created, the things he wants to reveal to us never change.

God never changes. He might have to speak a different language to tell *you* something about himself as opposed to someone in ancient Israel or medieval Europe or present-day India, but God is still God. He has always wanted us to know him and walk through life together with him, and he doesn't seem to have any problem telling us what we need to hear however we need to hear it. All that to say it would probably be a good idea for us to try to see whatever facet of God's character he was attempting to show Gideon. Why else would he have given us the story?

If I had to name just one thing that the story of Gideon is about, I would say it's about worship.

Start to end, this is a story about a God who wants his people to be awestruck at his power and majesty and to give him the glory and praise he deserves. It begins with the Israelites turning to the false gods of the nations around them. God then sends them into a time of trouble to help them see the correlation between worshiping the wrong god and life falling apart. They miss it for quite a while, but eventually they start turning back and crying out, and God has mercy on them. Enter Gideon, whose first mission is to tear down a pagan altar and use it to offer a sacrifice to God. Then, he is tasked with the incredible mission of driving out the enemies of God so that Israel could worship the Lord in freedom once again.

That task was the tipping point. God knew that right there, with the success of destroying their enemies, his people would either recognize his provision and give him the praise he had always been after or else pat themselves on the back and enjoy their "self-won" independence.

Isn't it likely that the latter is what they would have done? Isn't that what *we* do?

I pray and pray for God to give me a job so I can feel more like a man. He gives me one, and I go, "Man, it's a good thing I have such and such qualifications on my resume" or "Man, I nailed that interview!" as opposed to "God, thank you for this undeserved gift." Does that experience ring true for you?

We just have an astonishing ability to take the credit for things God does. Now, we love to hand God the bill when things don't go as we want them to (as did Gideon and Israel—see Judges 5 & 6), but when things go right it's all too easy to believe that we made it happen through our own perseverance, determination, skill, intelligence or whatever other good characteristics we may have. All of which have been given to us by God, of course, but we forget that.

It's not just us as individuals that do this, by the way. The church (the modern counterpart to the nation of Israel) also has a grand history of taking God's credit. We think our evangelistic programs are saving people, we think our talented worship team is bringing them to church and we think our Christianese self-help messages and books are making them better people. None of those things are necessarily bad, as long as we remember who is really doing the work. What if all we're really doing is providing people with a setting and a community in which to know God, and it turns out that's enough?

What if we could see that anything good we do as individuals or churches is God at work through us? And what if we worshiped him like that was true?

Isaiah, speaking from the other side of all the deliverance God authored through Gideon and the judges and David and the kings, said it this way: "Lord, you establish peace for us; all that we have accomplished you have done for us" (Isaiah 26:12).

Just take the time to read that again. It almost sounds like a contradiction at first, that everything we accomplish is actually God working on our behalf. But on second thought, what a paradoxical and wonderful way to live life! God has to be the one making us whole and giving us peace. And we don't have to sit around doing nothing while he does that, but we get to walk with him into the plans he has for us. It's actually the best of both worlds, not the worst. We work; he makes it *work*—but not necessarily in that order.

Jesus said the same thing: "I am the vine; you are the branches. If a man remains in me and I in him, he will bear much fruit; apart from me you can do nothing" (John 15:5). Two inevitable results, one from each side of one crucial choice: will we know Jesus and live with him, humbling ourselves before his sustaining power? Or will we try to make our own way apart from his strength? Success from one is just as certain as failure from the other.

Thankfully, it's not all on us. God gives us grace even as we make decisions that are only partially correct, and he works things to our good that we don't deserve at all. For example, I had a plan for my life that I laid out for God when I was about eighteen. It included, on a rough timeline, all the major events that were supposed to happen in the next few years. My timeline ended at approximately age twenty-five, by which time I was supposed to be a fulltime pastor, married, and have a young son and a house.

I am so thankful that plan failed. Don't get me wrong; I think those are some good goals, and I really did hit on some of God's desires for my life there. But I wasn't ready to receive them. Looking back, it's hard for me to believe how arrogant I was to put that all in front of God like he had to make it happen on my schedule. Honestly, the best punishment he probably could have given me was to let my plan succeed!

But that's not who he is. Instead, he loved me enough to let me try it on my own strength and fail so I would see how much I need to know him instead of just trying to use him for my plans. My girlfriend dumped me, my internship didn't result in a job, and the fragments of my plan slipped through my fingers. God loved me enough to take my plan apart piece by piece until all that was left was to trust in who I believed he was and obey him in whatever he gave.

That's kind of what he did to Gideon too. God didn't tell Gideon how to save Israel; he just told him to do it. So Gideon made a plan and summoned the biggest army he could muster, which seems totally logical. God never rebuked him for this action, but he also dismantled the plan completely by taking the army from 32,000 down to 300. Whatever plan of attack Gideon had thought he was going to implement before certainly wasn't going to work at that point! The goal, though, was still God-given and unchanged. Like I said about my plan, I believe I was hearing some of what God wanted for me and trying to accomplish it the best way I logically knew how. God has never rebuked me for this—he just made me fail. And I'm so grateful he did. Who knows what kind of arrogant monster I could have become if I had just gotten my way?

Back to Gideon: God had showed his power and mercy to Gideon, and now he was showing him the proper response. God's unraveling of Gideon's army and explanation thereof reveals something of his fundamental character. He insists on being worshiped. It is his prime value. He created the world for this purpose, so we experience the way things are supposed to be only as we worship him. But the blessings of a world in its proper order are the side dish, not the entrée.

God values his own glory above anything else, and he asks that we do the same. Not valuing our own glory—valuing his. This is only okay because he is God—there is no other reason good enough to make such a claim. Only he is worthy of such glory. As creatures, we don't get to decide why we were made or how

God should treat us. It may bother us that God doesn't care as much about our security or safety as his glory, but he doesn't, and he doesn't have to.

Gideon's story shows it clearly: God lovingly walked with Gideon through the whole thing, and he was truly concerned about Gideon's courage and security—but not so much that he let Gideon keep the whole army. That part of Gideon's mental comfort had to be sacrificed to the greater good of God receiving all the glory for the deliverance he was about to provide.

Gideon became a man by dangerously following God when it was clearly only for God's glory, not his own. The same is true for me and my generation. I am becoming a man only as my goal is not to find my own manhood and confidence but to know God and worship him. I don't just mean by singing or praying, either, although that has been a huge part of my walk with God. I can also worship God in the hard work that is part of manhood as I do it for his glory and not for my own plan.

God wants to give us the things of godly manhood and womanhood in such a way that it is clearly his work and results in his worship and his alone. Our own security and comfort will have to take the backseat. But we might just save a nation while we're at it. If we do, all we accomplish will be what God does for us. Are we willing to give God the glory of relying fully on his strength and not our own?

15. Her Own Strength

If you are one of those astute readers who actually remembers back to other parts of a book and tests it for logical contradictions, you may be wondering right now how we're supposed to reconcile walking in the strength we have (chapter 10) and relying fully on God's strength (chapter 14). It starts to make more sense as we realize the only strength we have to go in is God, but even so we may still feel uncertain of what we should do. The same One who told Gideon to "go in the strength you have" later tore apart the strength Gideon mustered so that "Israel may not boast against me that her own strength has saved her." So should we act boldly, or just wait for God to move? What are we supposed to do with this?

I believe this is primarily a question of focus.

It seems to me that most of us either make Gideon's mistake or Israel's mistake. God told Gideon to go in the strength he already had because Gideon was busy telling God he was too weak to do any of what God told him to do. God told Gideon to dismantle his army because God knew the people of Israel would claim the strength of victory for themselves if he gave them a standard military conquest. Gideon was held back by his doubt and fear; Israel had pride getting in the way. Do either (or both!) of those sound familiar to you?

It's tempting to view those two mistakes as opposite ends of a spectrum on which, if we could just find the middle ground, we could walk safely. The reality, though, is that both incorrect views are not so much looking at the wrong part of a picture as they are looking at the wrong picture altogether!

Think about focus. Both our pride and our self-doubt place the focus squarely on us. The two are equally deadly. Instead, God is trying to get us to look at him. That's why his paradoxical instructions to Gideon and Israel make sense together—both commands are meant to reveal not the proper way to look at the wrong thing but rather the right thing to look at!

In *The Purpose Driven Life*, Rick Warren gives what is probably the most helpful summary of this that I've ever read: "Humility is not thinking less of yourself; it's thinking of yourself less." In other words, don't waste your time trying to minimize or emphasize either your own strength or weakness. Instead, take your focus off of yourself completely and put it on God and what he can do. Don't look at a different part of the landscape of yourself; lift your head and look a completely different way!

Thankfully, God loves to help us with this process by bringing us into situations that vividly highlight our need of him. For me, just trying to grow up and become a man has been a situation like this. More recently, God has brought this incredibly beautiful woman across my path. I love being around her, but it constantly reminds me that I have no idea what I'm doing and I need God's help! How can I be a man that can lead her, someone strong and kind enough to earn her love and trust to the point that she would want to tie her fortunes to mine? If that happens, it will be a miracle, because my resources just aren't enough.

Speaking of insufficient resources, what about Gideon? Even though he surely knew he was still outnumbered, 32,000 men is a lot. With that many armed men milling around under your command, I'm sure you can't help but feel powerful. Maybe he even started to think he had a real chance of winning. But I'm sure that changed quickly when he only had 300. He certainly realized then that he needed nothing less than a miracle from God!

The important thing to remember is that, even though the numbers changed, God didn't create a greater need for himself by leaving Gideon only a tiny fighting force. He was just reminding them where the power was going to come from, just like he is reminding me I don't have what it takes without him. God was helping Gideon feel what was already the reality. He was trying to draw the focus to himself.

God's power is infinite. This is impossible for us to understand fully, but it means that any finite amount of power we possess stands in exactly the same proportion to his strength, no matter how much we bring (or think we bring) to the table. God is not too concerned with numbers or statistical probabilities in battle—he just decides who wins. Gideon could have had three million men instead of 300, and if God didn't fight for them he would have lost. This actually happens over and over in the Old Testament both for and against Israel, by the way. It doesn't matter which side has more people, only which side God fights for.

In fact, he doesn't even need to stage a battle. He could easily have destroyed all Israel's enemies with a plague or fire from heaven or any number of other ways. One time he even used bees (Joshua 24:12)! But whatever the method, he doesn't just want to be glorious—he wants us to *see* his glory and participate in it with him. Only as this happens do we really know from experience that the power is always his.

Jesus was the same way. He led his disciples out into a wasteland and then asked them to feed a huge multitude (see John 6). I'm sure they realized then that they needed his help, but do you really think the five loaves and two fish he got from the little kid made it any more or less of a miracle for him to feed the five thousand plus people there that day? God rained down bread out of heaven to feed thousands and thousands of Israelites in the desert for forty years. Did any human strength help Jesus feed the multitude? Of course not. It did, however, let the disciples (and the little boy!) participate in knowing God and his strength.

Five loaves, two fish, 300 men—it doesn't really matter what we bring to the table. Gideon didn't save Israel any more than that little kid fed five thousand people with his lunch, or any more than I can make myself into a godly man by my own strength. Our paltry gifts just serve as a reminder to ourselves and the rest of the world that any crazy amazing thing we seem to have done was accomplished by God's power in us (2 Corinthians 4:7).

God wants us to participate in doing his will, and the simple fact is that this is *always* more than we can handle. Sometimes we just see it more clearly than others. We might fall just a little short of being able to do what he asks, or we might only have some bread and fish, but we still fall short. God's power, on the other hand, is limitless.

Whatever we may feel like, we need God exactly the same amount every moment of our lives.

When we feel like we're on top of everything, we need him no less than we do in our most desperate moments. In our darkest hours, we're just realizing the ultimate reality: only in Jesus do we live and move and remain in existence. It doesn't take any more or less of Jesus' strength to become a man than it does to save a nation with 300 men. Our need for him is constant and complete.

Even though utter dependence on God is ultimately freeing, this reality can be difficult to walk in. Honestly, it is very hard to be continually faced with our desperate need. So we try to find ways around it.

Maybe we try to take God's blessings and run with them like they'll be enough to keep us going. "Thank you God for setting me free from such and such—that should be enough help and I'll take it from here" is how that one goes. We like to admit we need only as much help as it takes for us to feel fixed, and then we try to ride out the wave of good feelings God gives for as long as it lasts. A good name for this apathetic method of attempting to run from our need is coasting. It's one that keeps cropping up for me.

Unfortunately, the only way to coast is downhill. Yesterday's blessings will not be enough to keep me following the upward call of Christ tomorrow. I need to walk with him each day if I ever want to make progress, and that will bring me face-to-face with the truth that I can't do anything but slide slowly (or not so slowly) backward in life without his help.

Alternatively, if that's what it takes to make progress, maybe I'll decide that too much progress is just overrated anyway. Killing a dream is easier than living it—all it takes is a substitute of some kind that we think we can control and can convince ourselves is good enough as it numbs our hearts and distracts us into a dream world. Drugs, porn, video games, netflix, and social media seem to be common choices as zero-calorie dream substitutes. We often use these things or others like them to stifle our biggest dreams in life because those dreams are the ones that are too risky, the ones beyond our ability to make them happen, the ones that leave us with burning, aching longing in our guts and fear of failure in our heads. Dreams like that can be downright uncomfortable. Never mind that these are often exactly the dreams God has given us, partly because he wants to do amazing things through us and partly because he knows they will require us to face our need for him!

Things we don't know and can't control make us afraid, though. We're good at seeing situations coming that will bring our need to the forefront, and we often take different paths just to avoid them. I know I've suffocated my hopes like this. As I pursue God more, though, those big, risky dreams are coming back to life in me. It's exciting and a little scary, but I don't want to live without them anymore. If you have trouble sensing your need for God, it might be worth asking him if you've given up on any dreams that would cause you to need him. For example, the standard-issue American dream is really a very small one. It almost seems calculated to produce a life that falls under our own control, one that mutes our need for God and distracts us from true reality. Don't be surprised if what you *really* want is much bigger and less possible (for you).

Speaking of being distracted from reality, there is one more way I can think of that we try to run from our need for God. This one is much more insidious and thorny to navigate, but let me attempt it. In the church especially, I think we try to eliminate our need for God by replacing him with the rules he gave us. This is treacherous ground, of course, because he really did give us moral standards to live by that will help us walk in the life of blessing he intended for us.

But our salvation doesn't come from following the rules. It comes from trusting in Jesus, acknowledging our need for his perfect life and sacrifice. He gave us a new model for a good life: walk with me. Get to know me as a person through the work of the Holy Spirit inside you.

Jesus' model is more difficult than a list of rules. Where we subtly try to take needing God and walking in relationship with him out of the equation is where we try to take a set of rules we think are the most important and apply them to every situation. If we just have the rules, we don't see a need to keep asking Jesus what we should do or get to know him well enough that we gain his heart about sensitive subjects. Just apply the correct rule (or if the existing rules don't address a situation, make a new one!). We reduce a blessed life to a series of practical action steps that need to be taken (this is what most self-help books are) instead of embracing the vibrant but more demanding road of getting to know and becoming friends with the real person of Jesus—which it turns out takes just as much work and time as getting to know any other real person. When God does bless us, we try to reverse engineer the blessing and explain exactly what we did that "caused" God to pour out his blessing on us.

In short, we boast that our own strength saves us when we try to just follow the rules instead of knowing God. Not coincidentally, this is exactly what God was trying to prevent the Israelites from doing in Gideon's time. We've just replaced military strength with our own good deeds or church programs as the choice method of attempting to earn salvation and favor. Our pride then becomes the mask we use to hide from how much we need God's guidance and strength to actually accomplish anything. And as we try to walk by sight rather than by faith, we become increasingly blind.

Instead of all the ways we run from our need for God, God wants us to hold tight to those times when we clearly see our desperate need to know him and experience his mighty work. That way, we can carry this truth with us into the good times. Our need for him never changes, only our awareness of it. If we look at his strength instead of ours; if we learn to know his heart; if we let him shape us to remember our need and rely on him just as fully when things are going well as when we're in trouble—just imagine how we can surge forward in his power!

For example, say that through God's help I do become the man that wins the heart of the beauty I'm pursuing. I'll be on top of the world, but do I need God any less? It could all fall apart any moment without him holding us together. Sure, I will have received some of the blessing of God, but think how much more I could experience by continuing to rely on his strength. Who knows what amazing things we could do by consciously walking in need of God together over a lifetime?

The same strength that gets us out of desperate straits is also what propels us forward in good times. This power makes us men and women of God as we rely on it through every season. The strength we have to go in, the power to save a nation, is not ours. It's God's. Or rather, it is God himself—and he lives in our hearts. He has given himself to us. Will we take our eyes off our own pride and fear and look to him?

16. Anyone Who Trembles

If I had to pick out the one thing that has held me back the most in life, I would pick fear.

I know I'm not alone in that. The same fear I've seen in myself, I see in others everywhere I go. It hinders us in everything, from really investing our energy and working hard to taking risks in serving God and blessing others to talking with beautiful girls. I'm sure it's not just me; in fact, it's always been this way. Look how God took the biggest chunk out of Gideon's army: anyone who is afraid can leave. That took care of over two thirds of them!

Is part of you surprised when you read that? I know it was hard for me to believe at first that so many of them would leave at that announcement. I wouldn't want to be known as a guy who left because he was afraid. But what is the motivation behind that? Really, it's still just fear—fear of being recognized as fearful!

Fear is a powerful motivator. It can make us do things without much thought of any consequence but our own immediate safety. In fact, that's a primary characteristic of fear: it's all about us. This causes a bit of a vicious cycle. Fear comes from self-focus and the realization that it is beyond our power to protect ourselves. Then the fear causes us to focus even more on ourselves as we do whatever it takes to escape, even if it means leaving our brothers behind.

That's what Gideon's men did. Those 22,000 guys who left were already afraid as part of the larger army; I'm sure they weren't even thinking about how the 10,000 who remained were going to feel after they were gone! Their fear was so powerful and their self-focus so complete that they left guys who were probably their friends and relatives in a much more dangerous position. How could they do it?

Well, don't we do the same thing? It usually just looks different in our world where we don't often have to make decisions about joining life-or-death confrontations. Bear with me as I give what I hope is a pertinent example from my own life. I never lived up to my potential as a high-school basketball player, and it was mostly because of fear. I had some serviceable skills, but our coaches tended to use fear to motivate us, and they just generally made everything a much bigger deal than it really was. Sometimes they even kept notes on our mistakes during games—the truly egregious ones were rewarded with more laps or sprints at the next practice.

I see now that this was just high-school basketball, nothing to be afraid of. It wasn't even like normal high-school basketball, because I played for a tiny Christian school in a tiny league with far less importance even than the public school variety! It was, however, almost all our little school had going for it, and everyone made such a big deal out of it that I ended up with a game shaped by fear.

Fear is a fairly effective motivator for defense in basketball. It makes you alert and active, not wanting anything to slip through that could be considered your fault. I think I made the team mostly just by working hard and playing defense. Offense was a totally different story. On offense, I was paralyzed. I was so afraid of making a mistake (e.g. traveling, getting my shot blocked, etc.) that I basically tried to stay away from the ball. If it came to me, I would either pass it to a teammate right away or, if I was left *wide* open, shoot it immediately. Neither of these outcomes was considered a mistake. I was a reasonably good shooter, and everyone misses shots in basketball, so I couldn't really get yelled at even if I missed, as long as it was a good shot.

Why is that relevant to anything? It just puts a personal face on fear. In my self-centeredness, I had determined that I didn't have what it took to be a good player and earn the praise of my coaches, so I settled for avoiding their wrath. That made me a poor teammate because I was only trying to save my own butt, not looking for the best for the team. I could not have cared less if the person I was passing it to was in a good position to do something with it; I just wanted the ball (and the potential to mess everything up) out of my hands. Who knows how much better I could have made us if I hadn't been afraid to dribble and look for the best option?

Now (with apologies to anyone who doesn't like basketball for that long digression), can you see how that same kind of scenario could play out elsewhere in life? In your job, being too scared about your own position to help anyone else? In your marriage, worrying so much about getting what you think you need from your spouse that you forget about his or her needs? What about becoming a man or woman of God? Can we get so caught up in our own survival and prosperity that we miss God's plan (as well as the welfare of our brothers and sisters on the same road) entirely?

I say all this to point out that we are probably more like the fearful 22,000 than we realize. But I'm not necessarily holding up the 10,000 who stayed with Gideon after the first cull as the example for us to emulate either. I have a feeling they were afraid too, and possibly that a fear of man in being seen as a coward simply trumped their fear of death. That may sound crazy, but it's not that far-fetched. Keep in mind that fear of death is the *second* most common fear that people report. First place goes to fear of public speaking, a.k.a. fear of making a fool out of oneself in front of a big group. So that could very well have been what was going on. The story doesn't record any of them arguing when Gideon sent them away later on the fairly bizarre criterion of how they drank water out of a stream! It could be that the ones who wanted to save face were no less fearful than the others and just as thankful to have a chance to get out of there.

But I also point out our fears because I don't think never feeling fear is the standard we're meant to strive for. All of us are afraid sometimes for various reasons, and there's no point in beating ourselves up for it. The more important question to me is what we do with the fear we have. Or maybe a better way to put it is that what really matters is what *God* does even in the midst of our fear.

One of my favorite parts of Gideon's story is the way God helped him address his fears. We've already discussed God's powerful mercy in his first appearance to Gideon and in Gideon's tests, but again in this time of crisis God was personally concerned for Gideon. In fact, God knew that the "anyone who trembles with fear" category he had given included Gideon himself!

Finally, the night after God finished tearing Gideon's army apart, God told him to go down in the darkness and attack the enemy camp, over which he would be victorious. But first, God took the time to meet Gideon right where he was. God knew Gideon was afraid, so he told him exactly what to do if he was afraid to attack. *We* know Gideon was afraid because in the very next verse we see him following God's "if you're afraid" instructions!

I love following a God who does this kind of stuff. He saw Gideon, knew him personally, and loved him enough to set him up for success. It's his perfect love that casts out fear (1 John 4:18). I also love Gideon's response, though. No hiding from God—just a straightforward acceptance that the instructions for the fearful were exactly the ones he needed to follow. When I feel afraid, it seems easier to hide from God because I know I shouldn't be afraid if I believe in him and his mighty power. But what if I could just receive his love right in the midst of my fear like Gideon did and let his presence and reassurance cast it out? That is the road to victory.

Another thing I love about God's special instructions for Gideon's moment of fear is that he told Gideon not to go alone. God is the author of our faith, so he knows that it often grows exponentially when combined with someone else's. He also knows that we tend to second-guess what he tells us if no one else is involved in it. Perhaps God was especially concerned about this with Gideon given the episode with the fleeces discussed earlier.

And so onto the scene steps Purah, Gideon's servant, for his one and only appearance in the story (and the Bible). He snuck down to the enemy camp with Gideon (thereby risking his own life and doubling Gideon's chances of being caught) to hear, as it turned out, an enemy soldier's dream and its interpretation that God wanted to use to encourage Gideon. Then Gideon had no way around it—another sane person had heard God's assurance of victory, and it was for real. Purah's excitement probably added to his own and spurred him on even further. This is something totally different from the fear of man I supposed might have been keeping the 10,000 guys from leaving. Gideon wasn't going ahead with the attack to save face with his servant; he was experiencing the truth that it's much easier to be excited about something with someone than it is by yourself. Take it from an only child—I know. Because Purah was there, Gideon not only knew he had heard from the Lord but also could share his joy, an equally valuable blessing!

I may not have any servants, but God has certainly used this same strategy with me. He has been so faithful in giving me spiritual brothers and sisters who, when I am willing to risk sharing my fears and bringing them along with me on my spiritual journey, make me excited to go after God in new ways. They also let me know I'm not crazy when God is inspiring me to take risks in serving him and loving people. I don't know what I would do without this blessing. Well, actually, I've tried and failed to do things all by myself enough that I know a little bit of what it would be like and desperately don't want that outcome. Apart from God's help, though, I may never have experienced the blessing of following God with friends. Gideon didn't just decide on his own to bring Purah along, either. God specifically told him to do it, and for good reason. It's those seemingly little details that sometimes make the big difference.

Speaking of that, what happened after Gideon acknowledged his fears and experienced God's love in them? You might think I would say a victorious battle, and that was certainly one result. Even before that, though, Gideon did something that should not be passed over. As he received the message of encouragement prepared for him, Gideon worshiped God.

Right there in between the message and the victory, Gideon praised the Lord. No victory had happened yet. It was still 300 guys against 135,000. The difference was that Gideon finally believed in his loving God, and fear lost its power over him.

To become men and women of God is to learn to worship him before the victory he provides.

It's okay that we feel afraid. We even have the option to turn back and potentially miss part of the victory God is authoring. But if we learn to run to God instead of away from him when we are afraid, we can live in the love that casts out fear, just like Gideon did. Gideon's story is about worship, remember? Our stories are too. God is still calling our generation through fear and unbelief into wholehearted worship of him.

We don't have to wait until we feel like we've become the men or women we need to be. We may tremble with fear, but we serve a God who never does. His Spirit in us is one of power, not of fear. With him on our side, we have strength to enter the battle. What does it look like for us to worship him then?

PART IV

"Watch me," he told them. "Follow my lead. When I get to the edge of the camp, do exactly as I do. When I and all who are with me blow our trumpets, then from all around the camp blow yours and shout, 'For the Lord and for Gideon!'"

Judges 7:17-18

17. Watch Me

We worship God not just with our mouths but with our lives.

That may seem obvious, but it bears stating and re-stating as many times as it takes for it to really sink in. Singing a song with the band on Sunday morning is easy; directing your whole life towards God as a prayer is not. At least not for me. I help lead worship at my church, so the singing part feels natural to me, but leading worship means much more than leading songs! It actually means living a whole life that points to God and his glory, offering a sacrifice of praise that encourages others to bring their own as well.

If I'm right that the story of Gideon is very much about worship, then a big part of that theme is the way Gideon's worship changes. It starts with Gideon forming his own friendship with the Lord and praising God for his mercy to him individually. By the end of the story, though, Gideon starts turning outward. Once he hears the encouragement God has for him, he begins to worship in front of others. First, he praises God with his servant, and then he gets ready to lead his friends into the victory that will bring God praise.

And what does he say as he gets ready to let fly possibly the riskiest worship song/shout in history? "Watch me."

This is powerful to me, and not just as a display of confidence. This is Gideon saying, "I am going to trust God and live like what he said is true, and I'm not going to be quiet about it!" It's not arrogant—it's not about Gideon at all. He didn't tell them to watch because he was going to do something amazing. He wanted them to see him glorify God by taking the ultimate risk so that they would be inspired to do the same. As Gideon became a man, he went from a sidelong glance at God to a private dialogue with him to an outright example of how to praise him with a life—a worshiper unashamed and unafraid.

That's the kind of example I want to be. I don't want to live life in the winepress. I want to live in such a way that in every area I can look someone in the eyes and say "Watch me." But the only way that can happen is when all the different facets of my life are pointing towards God, reflecting his glory.

That's why we're told, "Whatever you do, do it all for the glory of God" (1 Corinthians 10:31), but this is a tall order. We seem to be born looking out only for our own interests, and our world certainly reinforces this tendency. All the advertising we're exposed to and the messages we see in the media teach us to value ourselves first and foremost. We grow up being taught to build our own little kingdoms.

Maybe (like me) you've said the Lord's Prayer enough times that the words have been completely divorced from their meaning, reduced to a pre-meal chant at family gatherings and such (by the way, a good cure for this is listening to the song "Your Love Is Strong" by Jon Foreman). It's easy to forget how radical it really is to pray to God, "*Your* kingdom come, *your* will be done." It goes against everything we grow up with, probably because there seem to be so few examples of people living like this (more on that later).

The examples we do see are often of selfishness, and if not that sometimes simply distraction. Our enemy is sneaky: rarely if ever will we hear him suggest that building God's kingdom is a bad idea. It's a wonderful idea of course, but what about getting this one little thing taken care of first? Just one more house repair project, a little bit of a better job, one more relationship... all the way down to one more funny video or internet meme. And so we slip slowly down into distraction and selfishness, like so many before us and around us, and we miss out on the kingdom of God. We selfishly and futilely try to make our lives like heaven and won't let heaven itself invade (which would actually fulfill our truest desires).

So we're talking about a fundamental paradigm shift here. It's all-encompassing. God is saying that in Jesus, we can break free from the hard-wiring of sin that causes us to view everything through the lens of how it benefits or affects us. We can fight the distractions of world and self and refocus our eyes and hearts on Jesus. Could it be that real blessing in life is found as we learn to see everything as it relates to God's kingdom and glory being revealed on earth?

If so, how do we even do that? No doubt about it, changing one's wiring is very difficult. I would go so far as to say impossible, actually, without God's help. But if we know he wants us to change in that way, it's safe to say he will help us do it. So how do we grow up into a generation of men and women who break out of small, hollow self-significance into the great mission and adventure of building God's kingdom?

It helps to remember we aren't the first ones trying to do this. Another young guy in the Bible who was trying to grow up was Timothy. The apostle Paul (same guy who wrote the simple but staggering "whatever you do" directive we've been discussing) gave Timothy some practical advice on how to make it happen. He said, "Don't let anyone look down on you because you are young, but set an example for the believers in speech, in life, in love, in faith and in purity" (1 Timothy 4:12). So if we want to stop being spiritual children, we need to start setting an example, not just for those younger than us but for anyone who sees any part of our lives at any time.

This "watch me" idea is important because if we think about setting an example, that forces us to consider what direction people are being pointed when they look at our lives. Do my actions and words point only to me, or are they directed at the larger goal of God's glory? This can be easy to overlook if we just do our own thing, but thinking about what others see in us shines a spotlight on who we really are glorifying.

Unfortunately, this healthy lifestyle is easy to confuse with a similar-looking one that is actually disastrous. It's so easy to spend way too much time thinking about what other people think of us and trying to manage their perceptions for our own benefit. I've done a lot of that, and actually when I say it's easy I just mean easy to slip into. It's actually extremely hard to do and takes a great deal of energy, enough to burn you out. But that preoccupation with the opinions of others is not what we're talking about here. I'm not sure we're meant to be concerned what people think of us at all, actually. Of course, that's not an excuse to hurt people or to devalue the insight of close friends. But no matter what people think of us, could they be drawn to think about and praise God when they see us? Now that's a worthwhile question.

I want my life, in all the areas Paul told Timothy about, to be filled with the confidence Gideon had when he told his 300 men to watch him. I want every aspect of my life pointing to God so that, if another believer were looking to me as a model, there wouldn't be any place where I'd have to say, "maybe don't really do what I'm doing here." And it's not because I care how any man judges me; it's because I care about God receiving the glory he constantly and exclusively deserves.

When I speak, I want to speak works of blessing and life. I want to build people up and encourage them, not tear them down. This can mean a variety of things for different people, but one personal example for me is avoiding sarcastic teasing. I tend to have an ironic (perhaps even acerbic) sense of humor, but God has been showing me that even jokes can sink in and leave scars sometimes, and I don't want to set that example for others. I don't need to cut other people down to get a laugh, and if I encourage them instead, they may well feel the blessing of God through that.

As I live my day-to-day life, I want to embrace hard work, enjoy God's blessings and take time to be with him in silence and stillness. This balance is so important, and honestly I've struggled with the parts of life that require diligence and sustained effort. God is convicting me now that this is an area where I couldn't encourage anyone to watch and emulate me. I'm learning to work because I want people to see God not only in how I rest in him or enjoy life but also in how I work hard for things that are important.

I also want to love unselfishly. I want to serve those who have no chance of paying me back. I hope to show my family and friends I care about them by what I do and say. I choose to love my girlfriend in a way that points her to God and looks to give before it receives. I want our relationship to be a model that other people in our situation can watch and see God in the way we relate. In all these things, I want to be consistent, just as God's love never fails.

I pray that my life will be filled with faith rather than with fear. For I have not been given a spirit of fear, but a spirit of power, love and self-discipline (2 Timothy 1:7). I want to believe that God can do great things, and by *believe* I mean *act like it's true*. There can sometimes be a strange unspoken pressure, even around other Christians, not to be too holy or pray too much or believe that God will do a miracle. If God is real, though, and really loves me, I haven't been asking for nearly enough. Gideon's confidence was well-founded: watch me believe God and lead us to victory. Surely nothing God is asking of me is harder than that! I want to believe his promises are true and receive his blessings, worshiping all the while. I think people will want to join me if I do.

Most of all, I want to follow God with a pure heart. My favorite prayer (so much so that I have it tattooed over my heart) is Psalm 86:11: "Teach me your way, O Lord; I will walk in your truth; unite my heart to fear your name." This singleness of mind and wholeness of heart is what it means to be pure, much more than just avoiding a certain list of things. This is my unceasing desire—to walk with Jesus in his way of truth as he puts my heart together to serve, love and point to him.

So these are the things I'm praying for. I know I'm not strong enough to change myself, but I believe God pays for what he orders and can give me the strength to glorify him with my life. I want to live in such a dangerous, confident and selfless way that I can say to anyone around, "watch me." Once they're watching, I want them to see Jesus and forget about me. What an example of godly manhood that could be! And what kind of impact could it make if we all started learning to live that way?

18. Follow My Lead

It's hard to even imagine how much good could be unleashed if we all simply learned to live our lives with the mindset of setting an example. It's something we all can do and grow into, and it happens on a personal, individual level. But there's a limit to how much impact we can make by ourselves. What happens when there's a problem too big to face alone, and we get to the point where someone has to stand up and say, "Follow my lead, we're doing _____"? Is this a pattern for all of us to emulate as well? I mean, there was only one Gideon and 300 other guys. What if they all tried to use his line?

It would have been a disaster. We all know what happens with too many cooks in the kitchen. Too many people trying to use their own recipe just makes a whole bunch of something that doesn't taste good and no one wants to eat. The same goes for leadership and planning—sometimes you just need one person with vision from God to lead people in a positive direction.

So what do we do with this as a whole generation longing to walk into the extravagant plans of God? Are only a few of us going to get to do the really awesome stuff while the rest just follow along or watch from the sidelines? Now, that's a straw man that's pretty easy to knock down. Of course God wants great things for all of us. He actually said that if we have faith in him, we would do even greater things than he did while he was here (John 14:12), which is mind-blowing. He clearly wants to give all of us power and vision. But when it gets to the most practical level, how can we all stand up and say "follow me" without spoiling the soup?

It's a complicated question, and one that Jesus' church really struggles to answer well. The model much of the church seems to have accepted goes something like this: Some people have a lot of wisdom and vision for God's work, so we need them to organize our programs. Some people have natural charisma and leadership ability, so we need them to run the programs. And every so often, there comes along someone who seems to have a good deal of both vision and charisma, and that's our Senior Pastor. He's basically in charge of making it all happen, knowing where we should go and motivating us to go there. The leaders of other ministries carry this same responsibility on a smaller scale in their own areas, and it all backs up to the S.P. in a big pyramid of authority.

I realize I'm being a little sarcastic. Forgive me. It's always easier to make fun of the things you grew up with, and this system is one of those for me. I don't mean to say that this common model is evil or wrong. Many great things have happened in many churches like this, and I don't want to disparage that. It may just be a flawed system that's the best we can come up with given the fact that all we have are flawed people to work with (kind of like pretty much every other large-scale system humanity has put in place, when you think about it)! I don't know, and I'm not saying I have the right answers or alternatives for all of this. The model we've got isn't necessarily bad.

It just isn't biblical.

Try as you may, I don't think you'll find the senior pastor pyramid model in the Bible. That doesn't mean it's *un*biblical, either—just that it isn't addressed in there either way. The Bible talks a good bit about overseers and administrators in the church, and I don't think anyone would dispute that some people are more gifted in these areas than others. It makes sense to have people in charge of areas that they're gifted in. The Scriptures are curiously silent, though, as to how to put it all together.

So what does that mean? Could it mean that there's not just one right way to do this church thing? Maybe Jesus wanted his church in different places and times to express all sorts of different ways of following him, just like each individual has their own gifts and calling, and just as Jesus himself did many different things while he was here! At the very least, I think it means our gatherings of Jesus-followers don't *have* to use the models we've been given. We can afford to look honestly at the flaws of our own churches and see what God might want to change. More than likely, we won't need to overhaul the whole thing. Tradition has value, and in many cases things become accepted because they just work.

But maybe some things do need to change. Could this generation be the one to say, "Follow my lead, we need to do this better/different/more"?

That long digression into church mechanics had a point, I promise. The point is this: some of the specific flaws of the church model I and many others in my generation have inherited are making it harder for us to become spiritual adults, men and women of God who can lead in a way worth following. I want to talk about those flaws, not to tear down the church but to offer suggestions on how to build it up stronger. I'm not saying that I know the answers, just that we're allowed to talk about this stuff.

And of course I'm not saying that all churches have these flaws, either. Some handle things better than others, of course—it's just that when the model I'm talking about goes wrong, this is how it seems to happen. Ok, enough disclaimers.

The biggest way I've seen that the pyramid church model goes wrong is that it tends to make church into a show put on by the gifted few for the passive many. People come to church ready to get their spiritual fix and get home in time to watch the Browns lose, hoping they get healed enough to survive it without cursing too loudly. The gentler, less sarcastic way of saying that would be that people come to church passive, ready to take in the music and sermon and prayer and maybe even receive any blessing God has for them, but not ready to build anything or offer anything other than perhaps a few dollars in the basket.

The thing is—why wouldn't they? The whole service is like a show, and we're used to being passively entertained. If no one is challenged or asked to participate, they'll probably continue just receiving from a few designated givers. I don't think that's healthy for either side! I dream of a church community where I could trust any member to get up and share, however briefly, something that God is showing them or working in their lives; where anyone could suggest a song for worship or offer a prayer for the congregation. Could it be done?

Of course, we probably shouldn't be entrusting important pastoral tasks to people who have no idea what they're doing. I'm just concerned that the system we have now might not ever challenge people to move past the "not knowing what you're doing" phase and take responsibility for their own spiritual lives. I do believe the common wisdom that in order to lead, you first need to understand how to follow. However, I also think following can become a crutch for those afraid or unwilling to lead in the areas of their gifting if they always know they can hide behind the show. Leadership comes more naturally to some people than others, but we all have gifts.

Unfortunately, many people with outstanding gifting will never get up and say "follow my lead in this" if they aren't encouraged to do so and given more involvement and ownership in the well-being of their church family. That in turn puts pressure on leader-types to always lead all the time and robs them of the chance to learn by following and submitting, which is instructive for all of us.

Church doesn't have to be like that, though. What if there was an ebb and flow of leading and following, serving and resting? What if we all agreed to discover the gifts God has given us and mutually support each other's leadership in the areas of our special gifting? Doesn't the body need all its parts to thrive? I don't know the logistics of how to achieve that, but just because it's difficult doesn't mean it's not worth looking into. Even if we don't change everything, how could our churches be more like that?

Perhaps one way would be for us to do more things together. Another unfortunate side-effect of the pyramid model is that it limits the amount of possible events. There is simply only so much stuff a select few people can put together. This can easily lead to what I would call an event mentality. A church can become centered on its events, usually the Sunday service and maybe a few others (Wednesday small group every other week, Saturday outreach first week of the month, etc.). The rest of the time, a church like this is little more than a fragmented collection of parts waiting to come to the next event.

What if our community was more like, well, community? What if we did more of the organic stuff of life together instead of just meeting for a couple hours every week? What if we devoted our whole lives to working together on the mission God has given us of sharing his great love with the world? If we did that, we would *have* to mutually support each other and let everyone lead, because there would be way too much stuff for just a few people to handle, even if it was their full-time job! Christianity was meant to be a lifestyle, not a collection of events. If we embraced this outlook together, maybe a greater part of a generation learning to be men and women of godly leadership could be encouraged to grow and bless the church with their gifts.

A great place to start moving toward community is just *doing stuff* together, both as young people and across generations. No event needed, just come along and serve God with me in such and such a way—simple, but potentially quite powerful. It just takes that little bit of extra effort to reach out. As we just spend time together, both in fellowship and in mission, those of us beginning to walk in leadership and gifting could just rub off on newer or younger folks (or even people who don't know Jesus or his kingdom yet) without demanding authority or position. Giving and receiving, growing together, leading from the middle and back, not just the front—that could make us people whose lead others want to follow.

While I'm on this topic, another flaw I've seen in the church model I've described is that it tends to burn out its leaders (even with the relatively few events on the schedule). It's hard to hear a message on service or evangelism and never see your pastor at the outreaches the church supports. For the pastors I've seen, it's not that they don't want to be there. They're just too tired from all the other responsibilities they have at the church to even make it. Also, they can start feeling like they have to be right and confident all the time because they're the leader. Not only can this lead to them stifling the dreams of aspiring young leaders who might have vision of their own (or driving them away completely), but it also can put a great deal of stress on the pastor or teacher. It's hard work having to be right and having things together, never feeling like you can show weakness or things might fall apart. No one should have to carry a weight like that, I don't think. Over time, it seems to get heavier and heavier.

The weight of the position also leads to an unhealthy cycle of leadership change in which a burnt out leader needs to find a new person to replace him/herself in order to keep the events or ministry going. Who better for the job than a young person with a lot of energy? This causes young leaders to be welcomed not into a healthy flow of following and then leading out, but into the same overload of constant leading that was killing their predecessors. Their energy sustains them for a while, but soon they too are burned out and the cycle continues.

I know it may sound strange given my young age, but I have already been through this cycle. In fact, I was pretty much burnt out on ministry at age 21, believe it or not. I don't share this to bash my church. Actually, I think my church is much better than average at helping people get connected in the life of the community. We may struggle a bit with the whole part where just a few gifted people do way too much of the work, though. No church is perfect—doesn't mean they're bad!

Anyway, I got put in charge of the high-school youth ministry while I was technically still supposed to be part of it—at age seventeen. I enjoy public speaking and teaching, I've been studying the Bible since I was a little kid, and I can play guitar. Perfect fit, right? So here I was, not even close to being or feeling like a man, and all of a sudden I'm a **leader**. Of course, my needy, insecure self was just soaking all this up, but really I still needed a chance to do a lot of following. I did learn a whole lot in this time of having to stand and ask people my own age and even older to follow me. But after about four years of it, I realized that I felt dull and distant from God and just way more tired than a 21-year-old person should be. I didn't feel like a man; I felt used by the system. It was a system made up of people who truly loved and cared for me, but it still ate me alive.

Maybe a more communal model could have prevented this. Maybe all I needed was someone to tell me not to let my own personal time with Jesus get swallowed up by asking him for material to share with the people I was supposed to be leading. Maybe I would've been too proud/insecure (see chapter 3) to ask for or receive help anyway, but I could have at least had a better chance! In any case, I offer my story as a caution to aspiring men and women who could be pressured to do too much leading and not enough following. I believe that deep down, all of us desire to have spiritual fathers and mothers who are ahead of us calling us forward, as well as people for whom we can be that person. As we grow into men and women of God, we want to be strong enough to stand and say "follow my lead," but we also desire the freedom to rest and support the leadership of others. Can we be confident and also humble enough to be a generation of that kind of leaders?

19. All Who Are With Me

Life is not all about leading and following. Yes, I know I just spent a whole chapter talking about those things and how important they are. It's not the whole story though. Sometimes, we want a chance to just be. We need time to just hang out, chill, process life or whatever you want to call it. I know I don't always want to lead or follow. So what happens then?

What seems to be the easiest way to escape from the system of leading and following is to go off by yourself and do your own thing. Our culture even reinforces this as normal—part of manhood in the movies often seems to include walking alone. It is very important that we have an individual walk with the Lord, and I believe there are things we learn in the quiet, lonely places with God (see chapter 2) that are for us alone. But it's simply a lie that we have to figure out how to be men and women in this world without anyone's help.

It's easy for this lie to slip into our thinking. I realized the other day that I've subconsciously believed my accomplishments somehow don't count for as much if someone helps me do them—as if we can do anything without help! That's a really stressful way to live. It's hard enough to succeed at most important things without any help, but you might actually have to actively stop people from helping you if you want to feel like you did it all yourself! This is foolishness, of course, but our pride and selfishness can run that deep.

Don't you long for something better than that? I do. I don't always want to lead or follow anyone, but I don't want to have to figure life out by myself either. What is this longing that runs even deeper than my prideful independence or my desire to lead and be led? What I'm looking for is *community*.

Community might be something of a vague word, but what I mean by that is just people who will truly be with us. I don't mean people who are just present in the same places we are or even necessarily people with whom we do basic life stuff like working or working out or purposely *not* working. I mean that we are (or at least I am) deeply desiring people who will really be *with* us—for us, on our side, willing to trust us and walk with us through whatever life's path may hold. I'm talking about something totally aside from leadership status as well. Maybe we'll walk a bit ahead of our friends at times; maybe they'll be pulling us along other times. Mostly, I think we just want people with whom we can walk together.

That's what Gideon's band reminds me of. Sure, he was the leader of the group, but it seems that the small force God left him was completely committed to him. They were with him, for him, and trusted him unequivocally. Just think how much trust it took to follow this plan Gideon laid out for them— we're going to walk up next to the enemy camp, spread our tiny, massively outnumbered force out all around it and then start screaming and blowing trumpets. That was it. And you know what? They all did it! Why?

I'm sure they all respected Gideon's leadership, of course, but that's the kind of leadership decision that can lose you people's respect in a hurry. Maybe they trusted God more than the average joe, but given the spiritual climate in the land at the time that seems unlikely too. Something else had to be at play there. Now, the Bible doesn't tell us anything about the demographics of Gideon's 300. I imagine that some were older than him, some younger, but I bet they all had one thing in common. They followed Gideon on his seemingly crazy and suicidal mission because it was their mission too. They were fighting for their families and their nation and their futures. They were trying to be men who could look at themselves in the mirror without being ashamed. They were men looking for the freedom God has for each one of us, and they were willing to stake their lives on it.

They did it together. "Each man held his position," the story tells us (Judges 7:21).

That inspires me. Is there some equivalent we can find to this in our age? It's unlikely that we'll ever have to surround and storm an enemy camp, but isn't modern life a battle enough? With all its constant temptations and pressures, our day requires a band of brothers just as much or more than any other! That makes me very confident that God still wants to give us community, people we can look at and call "all who are with me."

One place this can come from is family. Our biological families can be our greatest allies—or our closest enemies. Of course, some people have terrible or abusive families, and I think God would have those people look elsewhere for community unless he does some serious healing. For a lot of us, though, we have a family where there is a longstanding love; it's just often mixed with equally longstanding frustration. Our families know us well, but often only as we used to be. Maybe if we could leave the past behind, though, and see our family members for who they are now while trying to show them who we actually are, we might find that some of the fellow travelers we've been looking for have been right under our noses the whole time.

I also think God gave us marriage in part so that many of us will have at least one person who has actually *promised* to be with us. Isn't that what the marriage vows are all about? Better or worse, richer or poorer, sickness and health—it's all about two people telling each other, "We're in this together, and I'm not giving up on you just because you hit a rough patch. From here on out, we're on the same side no matter what." The mutual safety and security this affords when two people really mean it is a very powerful thing. It isn't good for us to be alone; even one person we can count on to be truly with us and for us makes a world of difference. Combine this with love and trust and you have a force that equips people to take on the world.

Regardless of our family situations, though, there is one avenue of community that is open to literally everyone. I'm talking about friendship, and not just the kind where you do activities together and never really talk (although that's fine), but the kind where you actually invite someone into the real stuff of your life. This is a big reason why God gave us the idea of church. He could easily have commanded that we all relate to him individually and not worry about anyone else, but instead God's heart is for unity and a band of believers drawing near to him together. He did give us all the same mission, after all. It makes sense that we would be much more capable of accomplishing it together.

I'm not saying, by the way, that you can't have friends who don't share your beliefs or go to the same church as you. What I am saying is that the extent to which you're on the same mission with someone greatly affects how much true community you can have with them. That's why I would encourage those looking for a church not to pick necessarily the one they think is the most correct or spiritual or doctrinally sound but one where they can connect with the people in heart and vision and see themselves working on the same mission in

God's love. If the church has visible flaws (and I don't know of any that don't), fine—maybe your gifts are the ones they've been missing! God wants to give us community this way—why not take him up on his offer?

It's not enough to just find some people you want to walk with, though. For anyone to really be with you, you have to be with them. That means not only supporting them but also letting them see what's really going on with *you* (good and bad), which is actually much harder than being supportive for many of us. This is not all about us, remember. It's about becoming men and women who glorify God, and this is one way we can do it. He designed community, and we honor him and help his plans move forward when we pursue it.

That's what God led Gideon to do. First, he whittled the army down to a small, close-knit group of warriors (who were probably also a little crazy). Then, he helped Gideon walk with them in community. God told Gideon to invite his servant, Purah, into his moment of fear by having him come down to the enemy camp and receive God's encouragement with him (see chapter 16). Then Gideon also shared the good news with the camp before they set out to attack: "The Lord has given the Midianite camp into your hands" (Judges 7:15). They didn't have to follow him blindly because he learned to let them know what was going on.

So it's not easy, this community thing—but it can be done, in family and in friendship.

Family can be especially tough to change into community. Maybe there are long patterns of poor communication or just a sense that certain roles and ways of relating will never change. Maybe there's love, but it feels trapped under fakeness and shallow conversation. It makes the move towards authenticity and real love seem risky. It is a real risk. But isn't it also possible that your family members would be blessed to know who you really are and rise to the occasion in support? It might take time—I know I've had my share of battles with my family as I try to become a man, and sometimes I made the situation worse by not treating them with the respect they deserve. As I've shared real stuff with them, though—struggles, victories, apologies—they have been able to do the same. They love Jesus, and we're on the same mission now. In fact, my parents are some of my closest allies and have never failed to support me in any way that I've needed. That's a miracle, and by that I mean that God did it. He can do the same for you. Family and community were both his ideas.

I'm not married as I write this, so I don't exactly feel qualified to comment on how to foster community in marriage. I do, however, have a wonderful girlfriend, and being with her is teaching me a lot. By this point in our relationship, I've shared with her some things I'm proud of but also some things I've been really ashamed to say. The amazing thing about it, though, is that as I've shared even these things I feel might cause rejection, she has offered acceptance and love. She even said it makes her feel closer to me that I would share like that, and that it makes her feel safe to be herself and share her own story. It blows my mind, honestly, but it's so wonderful. I don't really know what else to say about that, except that that's how God loves us. (Also, I think it's safe to say that if you find someone like this, he or she is a keeper!)

Friendship community can be difficult to find too, in part because there are so many people and it's hard to know where to start. It can be so tough to break through the surface layer of shallow conversation where everyone seems to linger. Sharing real things isn't easy! It's hard to know when is the right time and who are the right people. The fear of rejection is real, but the possibility of finding someone who will be with you as a fast friend is just as real. Again, it doesn't happen all at once. Many of the friendships God has blessed me with are so longstanding that I don't wonder anymore if those friends are truly on my side or for me. They've proved it by being there through my crazy and rough times, and hopefully I've done the same for them. Friendships like this are worth the risk of being vulnerable and open with people.

Let me share a story that explains this better than I could otherwise. I told the story earlier of how I learned to ride a bike at seventeen and a couple of the crashes that ensued. I know how to ride now, but my late start has left me not nearly as competent a bike-rider as my friends are. Still, I let some of them convince me to go on a 40-mile ride with them a few years ago. I borrowed a crappy bike with bad brakes and set out on the trail with them.

I was about as tense as could be the entire time, constantly worried about crashing with this hard-to-control bike that wasn't even mine under me. It didn't help that we were riding on the Erie Canal towpath trail where you don't really crash—you just go straight into the canal if you go down (or so it seemed to me). I fought it out for about twenty-one miles, but then I had to pass someone on a bridge. All my fears were realized as I clipped the side rail of the bridge with my handlebar and went down in a skidding heap with a couple nice bruises, a patch of missing skin, and several splinters from the wooden bridge for good measure. Well, almost all my fears—I didn't end up in the canal. But I'm not proud to say that the next thing that happened was that I threw (literally) the bike against the bridge and quit the ride in frustration.

What happened after that, I'll never forget. First, one of my friends offered to quit the ride too, and he ended up sitting with me and my sullen attitude the whole time while our friends finished the ride and came back with the car to pick me up. My best friend tried out the bike I'd been riding and said he probably would have crashed it too. And then—the coup de grace: that fine French phrase literally means "stroke of mercy," which could not be more perfect in this case. Another friend (who was really just my friends' dad at the time but is now a friend of mine) looked me right in the eyes and said, "You really went for it today!" with a warm smile.

It's hard to explain what happened at that moment. I wanted to hide in the shame of my wreck, but he saw the risk I'd taken and commended me even in my failure. It still makes me want to cry when I think of it now, but my initial reaction was visceral and very different: I had the powerful urge to punch him right in the stomach and take the wind out of those sails. I felt my fist clench. But I couldn't move, or even speak—the sharp stroke of grace had already sunk into my heart. I knew without a doubt that God had just spoken to me through that kind man. God loves us in success or failure, and that's the love my friend showed me that day. He was *with* me in that moment, whether I wanted it or not. Deep down, I really wanted it.

That's true community, and it helps us become the men and women we need to be. I'm so thankful for what God has allowed me to taste of it, and I'll never be the man he's calling me to be without it. It's worth finding at any cost or risk. And just think—what would a whole church of people who could call each other "all who are with me" be like?

20. From All Around the Camp

According to the most recent census, approximately 1,265,000 people live, like I do, in Cuyahoga County, Ohio. This is the county where Cleveland is, for those who aren't from around here. If you're wondering how that has any bearing on Gideon or becoming a man, just hold on—I'll bring it around. But first, here are a couple more statistics.

The percentage of people in America who go to church each week is a topic of much debate. Even though about 70% of Americans identify themselves as Christian, I've seen claims as low as 25% and as high as the mid-forties for church attendance. Say we go pessimistic and decide that it's only 20%, and then we only count three quarters of those to account for religious attendees who aren't Christians. That still leaves about 189,750 churchgoing Christians in this county, mathematically speaking.

That is a lot of people. Surely a group of people that size in such a small area could accomplish any mission they set out to do! That many people with Jesus' mission of loving the poor and sharing the good news—what could stand in their way? What could possibly derail such an incredible force?

One idea: break it into 1,270 parts which, for the most part, have no idea what the other parts are doing. That might do it. Guess how many churches there are in Cleveland? My quick search of yellowpages.com says 1,270 just in Cleveland, not even counting the rest of the county, where there are certainly many more. Even that conservative estimate only leaves about 150 people per church. Suddenly the unstoppable force doesn't sound so impressive anymore. Gideon had twice that many!

Honestly, 150 per church sounds a little high to me. There are a few really big ones that skew that number upward, but for every one of those there must be about seven tiny storefront churches with 25 people. Seriously, these little things are *everywhere* in Cleveland. I'm sure this is an issue in other cities too, but I just happen to know firsthand that it's epidemic here. Cleveland has long been a city of division, and the churches show it. Maybe that has something to do with why we're the second-poorest big city in America. Maybe it's even connected to the greater Cleveland area becoming the heroin overdose capital of America. The point is, the mission Jesus gave the church is not being accomplished here. God, forgive so many of us for doing so little!

Speaking of America, Cleveland is just a microcosm of the Christian church nationally and internationally. Even though modern communication should make unity easier than ever, the worldwide church body struggles to connect its various parts and fulfill its mission. Why are Christians world-famous for division and infighting rather than acts of love and service? I believe this lack of unity is the devil's greatest victory in the church. Division is his trademark, right from the day he first brought separation between Adam and Eve and the Lord. I also believe it's killing a generation that should be growing up into the next men and women of God.

The people of my generation long to be part of something bigger than ourselves. That's why we pay the highest prices in history to go see concerts and sporting events, even though the internet has made it possible to watch or listen to pretty much anything you want right from your home, with arguably a *better* view and sound quality than being there live. We want to be caught up in something important, and we want to do it with our friends.

This is exactly what the church could be offering. We've been given the biggest, most important mission ever, and it's a community mission. Sadly, though, our churches seem small and their events and outreaches insignificant. From what I've seen and heard from others, there's little to no sense of the larger vision of Jesus in far too many churches. Maybe we're too busy with our little events to see it.

Let me try to shift gears here. I see the current picture of Jesus' church as sobering, but I don't mean to be overly bleak. There are many churches that walk in unity and really do work on the mission of Jesus, accomplishing real things for his kingdom and not their own. I also don't mean to say that small churches are a bad thing. Many people find Jesus in the close-knit community that kind of ministry offers, and Gideon's story is a prime example of God using small numbers to do big things. However, I believe much of the division and smallness in the church in our day comes from the enemy, not from God. It results from worldly thinking and pride, not the humility and unity we need. What we don't need is a bunch of massive churches competing with each other through big, flashy events for the same already-Christian people. We also don't need another gifted leader to take his twenty-five people to a new storefront, thinking he's Gideon when he's just supposed to be one of the 300 guys around the camp.

Speaking of Gideon, let's get back to him for a bit. That statistical decimation of the church I just went through reminds me a lot of what happened to his army. But what God left him with, as we saw in the last chapter, was a highly unified band of devoted followers. God then used that tiny group to do the immense task he had in mind. So it can happen! In fact, Gideon broke his small group into three even smaller segments that he stationed all around the enemy camp. But these three groups were really still one. They all walked in unity, and they all raised the same shout. They were in communication, and they were all on the same page with Gideon's plan.

Any chance we have of fulfilling God's mission for his church starts the same way—with unity at every level. Yes, we'll need a Gideon or two. Just as importantly, though, we need people who believe in unity.

The Bible tells us that the whole point of God giving his gifts to us is "to prepare God's people for works of service, so that the body of Christ may be built up until we all reach *unity* in the faith and in the knowledge of the Son of God and become mature, attaining to the whole measure of the fullness of Christ" (Ephesians 4:12-13). Do you hear that? We will never reach the full maturity God has for us without walking in unity in the faith and inviting others to know Jesus with us! True godly manhood and womanhood are impossible without unity.

It has to start small, though. Just like Gideon's little band of warriors walked in unity as each man held his position, we need to stand for the harmony and peace of whatever small family we find ourselves a part of. It doesn't matter if your church is 25, 150, or 1,700 people—unity begins right there.

This is a big deal to God. It's also especially important to me personally—I told the story in chapter 6 of how a church split almost derailed my faith journey early on. When churches get divided, whether by gossip, doctrinal squabbling, irresponsible sins of leaders or whatever else, it sends a clear message to young believers in and around them. It tells them the community and vision they're looking for won't be found there. Barring divine intervention (as in my case), they *will* look elsewhere for it. Unfortunately, the other places they look won't lead to manhood either, and this is the story of far too many in my generation. It's up to us to help write something different for the next one by keeping our churches unified.

One step in this direction—men and women of God have no place for gossip. Don't even listen to someone tear down a leader or pastor or anyone else in your church. Unity is too precious. Spend time talking *to* people, not about them. If you have a problem with someone, don't just leave—be part of the solution! Young men and women need this kind of safe environment to grow up into the new leaders of the church. It's hard enough to do without having to worry that someone is going to abandon you or tear you down at any moment!

Another unifier—value people over doctrines. Love is of paramount importance, not correctness. Someone can come to your church and be a real Christian without believing all the same things you do! We can have disagreements and still love the same Jesus, and churches don't have to be divided along the lines of who believes which lesser doctrine. Of course, there *are* some non-negotiables. The Apostles' Creed provides a good list, but you'll notice it's fairly short. It's important that I'm *not* saying we have to affirm people like the ones who hold up "God hates gays" signs at people's funerals; What I am saying is just that the church is so divided right now that we can't even form a united front against those nutjobs to say to the world, "Hey, those signs are not Christianity!" We fight over too many little things for people who agree on the big ones. Being a Christian isn't all about being right anyway—it's about being loved and what happens after that.

One more point of unity—our churches need a culture where people don't have to feel ashamed to openly repent and discuss their failures. For the most part, I don't think the big secret sins we find out about and lose gifted leaders over happen suddenly. They happen when people learn the habit of hiding. I propose that we can never be the men and women we need to be if we have to hide every failure for fear of being shamed. Try to make your church a place of openness. Call sin what it is, but remember we've all done it and don't think less of people when they confess and repent. Don't condemn people; point them to Jesus. He's already claimed exclusive rights to final judgment anyway, which is fantastic news because it means the only person with the right to take us down is also the one who loves us the most out of anyone ever.

If we had some more churches that were unified like that, maybe the world would start to take notice! Those kind of churches would be well-positioned to join forces and start accomplishing the larger mission too, don't you think? The same principles apply to unity between churches.

What if, instead of trying to convince people our church is the best, we spent time pointing out anything great we see in other churches? What if we, still believing what we believe in faith, shifted our outward focus onto the big, non-negotiable doctrines of Christian orthodoxy and were willing to work together with anyone who shares those core beliefs? What if we admitted where our churches are weak and looked to partner with churches that are strong in those areas?

In fact, what if anytime we see a need or feel a calling to a mission, we looked first to see if there's someone already doing it that we could partner with? Maybe there's a Gideon already blowing a trumpet, and we need to stand up around the camp and join with him. Here in Cleveland, we've started collaborating with prayer meetings and a worship summit where people from about 20 churches in the area (only 1,250 to go!) have come to worship God and pray for our city. Even though it's still not that many people who have caught the vision, it's been wonderful. These churches are as different as can be, but it's awesome how the leaders of each have put differences aside and worked together. It makes me think that if we could be humble enough as leaders not to have to be in charge of everything, maybe then we could start seeing the big change and vision that a new generation of godly men and women is longing for—and we could grow up into it together.

What if, in our day, God is not giving us Gideon's tiny force but a huge one just waiting to come together? What if we have enough already to end the heroin epidemic in Cleveland? The city would have to stand up and take notice! Such a unified victory would be enough to cast all our petty divisions to the background, washed out in the overwhelming light of God's glory. We could have unity all around Jesus' camp. What kind of a shout could we raise if we did?

21. Shout

When was the last time you shouted?

It might seem like a strange question, but think about it. How long has it been? What was the situation? How did you feel afterward? Was it a good experience?

I ask all that because there seems to be something inside each of us that wants to shout. I live across the street from an elementary school, and I do a lot of my work (writing and editing) from home. Most of the time, the school being there has no impact on my daily life. But then there's recess. Between about 11am and 1pm, Monday through Friday, the sonic atmosphere of my neighborhood is very different. The symphony of shouts, screams, shrieks and howls that floats through my windows each day is quite consistent. It's not like some days they yell and some they don't. Every single day the weather is good enough for them to be outside, the sound is pretty much the same. They never get tired of it; it's how they express themselves and have fun.

I'm actually not really annoyed by it. I've discovered that particular block of time is not the most productive one for me anyway, so it's a nice time for a long lunch break and a walk with the Lord. Adult lunch breaks are a very different thing from recess, aren't they? Beginning right at the age of those little kids across the street, we start living in a culture that is bent on getting us to be quiet. It becomes culturally inappropriate to express ourselves in anything but an "inside voice," to quote the phrase we use on our children. God is in the silence too (see chapter 2), but what about that urge to be loud? Does it go away as we age? Or does it just get stifled?

I don't think it goes away. In fact, it pokes its head out in a few socially acceptable scenarios for yelling. Take sporting events for example. Americans have decided that it's ok to shout when you're at the game (or even scream at your TV while you watch the game), but only when something good or bad happens to "your" team. In other countries, people (soccer—ahem, football—fans especially) take it to the next level and just yell, chant and sing right through the whole thing. No one thinks any of this is all that weird, or if they do at least no one stops all these people from going back to their normal jobs and lives the next day like nothing happened.

Concerts are another one. We admire performers who sing with passion and power. Maybe we even learn the words so we can go to the concert and sing along with them. We cheer for them to come out on stage. We cheer again when they "leave" the first time so they come back for the encore. Then we go home talking about how great it was, even though the reality is that we've heard far better sound quality on our stereos at home, and the volume was actually so uncomfortably loud that it takes three days to feel like there's no more cotton in our ears. There's just something about being there, though—it releases something in us.

What is it that gets released? Well, I'm no psychologist, but I think it's a desire to be caught up in something bigger than ourselves. Another way to put that: it's worship.

Think about it. All of the times we let ourselves be loud are about things bigger than ourselves. It's about the team or the music or, for the recess kids, just the joy of running around outside or the adrenaline of being chased. By the way, they don't just go off by themselves and yell; they do it together as part of a game or contest or whatever else it is that is clearly the most important thing in their world at that time. Adults aren't so different. Sporting events and concerts and such are about experiencing, in community, some taste of the bigger issues of humanity—the injustice of life (a missed call by the referee), the beauty of the world (an incredible solo or perfectly executed play), the sting of our personal failure and defeat (especially if you're a Cleveland sports fan), and so on. They just let us get loud about it.

Now let me be clear that I'm not saying cheering for a sports team or a band is (necessarily) idolatry or wrong worship. I *am* saying that true worship of God is the ultimate expression of what all these other things are just a shadow of. We all have deep feelings about what happens in our lives: joy, heartache, anger, fear, excitement. We know other people feel these things too, even if they aren't showing it. We're just looking for the context of something much bigger than our own selves to let these big things be expressed. We're looking for God—for worship.

Worship as God designed it is where we get to bring, together with a loving community who feels the same things, our deepest and strongest feelings before the One who is bigger than us by the greatest amount possible, and where we can express all these things in a way that physically mirrors their intensity inside us: by getting **LOUD**. God doesn't just permit us to do this; he invites it! It's what we were made to do.

No emotion is off limits to be brought before God as worship, no matter what the modern church or Christian radio may model for us—just read the Psalms. In fact, the whole Bible is full of this stuff: Make a joyful noise, come before God with singing and drums and trumpets and whatever else you can find, cry out in the day of trouble, lift up a shout of victory, pour out your frustrations, raise your voice, sing with all your heart, awaken the dawn! All these things we feel so deeply and search so desperately to find any outlet to express, God invites us to offer to him in prayer and song and shout—in worship.

This is incredible, when you think about it. Why would the God of everything want to be bothered with all our relatively insignificant emotions and life situations? Maybe it's because our coming to him brings him glory. He receives glory not because we feel some certain way but because, regardless of what we feel at the time, we're coming to him. He made us to do that, and it shows his greatness when we fulfill our purpose. When we worship, we're also telling God that he's bigger than whatever it is we feel—joy or sadness or anything else, he's the only one who can help us deal with it. He's the only one who can handle our uninhibited emotions, and he welcomes us to pour them out.

I'm starting to realize that whatever my emotions are, just telling God about them and offering them to him is worship. Expressing them through song is really helpful for me, but people do it in different ways. The key thing is that the simple step of coming to God with what we think and feel shifts our focus in a way that we may not even perceive. If we decide to worship God, the very act of doing that turns our eyes off ourselves and puts them on God. Then we can tell him how great he is regardless of what a mess we are! It's not that our problems or victories go away; it's just that we're looking to someone much bigger, and he loves us. This shift of focus is the essence of worship, and in it God is glorified.

Don't you think that's what was happening with Gideon and his men? For them to raise the shout they did, their eyes had to be looking somewhere other than themselves. Focusing on their paltry fighting force would only have left them afraid. Gideon knew where to look, though. Right before they took up attack positions, he told his troops "Get up! The Lord has given the Midianite camp into your hands" (Judges 7:15). He didn't say to move so they could prove themselves or because they were going to win—it was because of the Lord. God had to be what they were looking at, or they never would have done what they did. With their gaze on him, though, they offered a shout of victory as worship. The outcome of the battle totally aside, God was glorified in that moment.

I made the claim earlier that the story of Gideon is really a story about restoring true worship. It's a story of God turning the eyes of a whole people off of other gods and their own troubles and back to himself. They hadn't necessarily forgotten about God; they just started trying to give some of his praise to someone else, and God refuses to share his glory. In fact, Gideon himself later stumbled by trying to share God's glory (Judges 8:22-27). He did well by saying God should rule Israel when they tried to make him ruler after his victory, but then he messed up and tried to take just a little of God's glory in the form of gold, which ended up becoming yet another idol that blemished the victorious peace God gave. God's goal and our freedom are both all about right worship. What do we look at besides God that stops our shouts in our mouths?

Maybe we have some idols of our own. Anything we put our focus on instead of God could qualify, not just a literal false god. We put a lot of focus on love, money, possessions, and things like that. It's not that these are bad, but when our focus is on them it makes our world small. We can only live as big as whatever we're looking at. Even the most beautiful woman, the best job or the biggest house is not even close to big enough. That's why God wants our eyes on him.

I have a feeling, though, that the main thing we look at instead of God is just ourselves. As a worship leader, I see this on the faces of the people I'm called to lead in worship each week. It's such a battle to enter into worship without looking at ourselves and where we've failed or succeeded—as if that has any bearing on God's love for us. I also see people fighting their obsession with what others think of them—what will I look like to my friends if I really offer my uninhibited worship to God in all the emotions that might entail? I don't mean to be too hypothetical here either: I struggle with these things too! Will people respect me as a leader if I really let go and praise God with all I have and am?

I forget, though, that the end goal of leading worship isn't for people to respect my leadership—it's for God to be glorified. If he wants a shout, he can have one! The things I feel inside are certainly strong enough to merit being loud, and he deserves to have the real me. If I can shift the focus off myself and onto him, I will have succeeded. Paradoxically, it's this same focal shift that will lead us into becoming the men and women of God in a new generation. When we don't look at ourselves, we can shout in victory before the battle and then see God accomplish it for us.

My own manhood has never been about me at all.

It's about God's glory from start to end. And that means it includes more than just singing and shouting too. A life of worship isn't one of constant song but rather a God-focused life of purpose and power that reverberates across the land, echoing like deep calling to deep in the roar of God's waterfalls (Psalm 42:7). Is your life loud like that? Can people hear your worship in all you do? I want to live in such a way that it would be noticeably quieter if I was gone. That kind of shout can only go up as I learn to fix my eyes on God in every situation and let the king of the earth receive the glory he deserves.

Like Gideon's, it will be a risky shout. Things could go wrong, and immediate victory is not assured—only a life that is fully alive through our God who has given us more than enough evidence that he can and will back up his promises.

Will we trust God to make us men as we lift the shouts of our hearts to him alone in worship? What kind of weapon could we be in his hands if we do?

22. A Sword for the Lord

Men love swords. I know some women who like them too, but it's pretty much universal for men. If my sweeping claim doesn't seem as self-evident to you as it does to me, try this experiment: pick any two little boys you can find, and give them each a stick. I'd bet money that within two minutes, probably within thirty seconds, you'll be watching a sword fight. Also, what common ground do classic "man movies" of my generation as diverse as *Lord of the Rings*, *Star Wars*, *Gladiator*, and *Braveheart* all share? Sword fighting. It doesn't matter if it's a claymore, a scimitar, a light saber or Andúril itself—men love this stuff. Even the names are cool.

Becoming a sword for the Lord sounds pretty manly. It's no surprise that this phrase was coined by a group of 300 men. Gideon actually didn't tell them to say this, by the way; he just wanted them to shout "for the Lord and for Gideon" (Judges 7:18). The warriors God had chosen added the sword part themselves. It must have sounded stronger to shout. Incidentally, I would also have accepted "epic shouts" as a correct answer for what all those movies I just mentioned have in common. These things are just what happens when you put a bunch of guys together.

Deep down, guys reading this are getting a little excited now. It excites me too—I get to be a weapon for the Lord! I wonder what kind of sword I am. How many battles will I win? This is what men want manhood to be all about. Before we get too far ahead of ourselves, though, we have to remember what a weapon really is. A sword is just an instrument, a tool used by its wielder for a specific task. It doesn't swing itself.

Speaking of instruments, I play guitar, and that's the closest thing to a weapon that I wield. Sometimes when I play and worship God, I feel like I'm doing battle with the spiritual forces of evil that Paul talked about (Ephesians 6:12). My bass guitar feels especially weapon-like to me: it's big, heavy, shiny, and makes sounds that can shake the whole building I'm in (with the right equipment)—but only if I play it. It's a weapon, but it has no power just sitting in its case in my room like it is as I write this. It has to be in my hands.

A sword is the same way, right? The only way it's doing any damage lying on the ground trying to swing by itself is if somebody trips over it. It has to be in the hands of a warrior to become a true weapon. I'm sure you see where I'm going here: manhood is no weapon at all if we try to do it ourselves. My own manhood is not about me at all. In fact, it's all about dying.

"I have been crucified with Christ" is how Paul put it (Galatians 2:20). Do we really have to trade our chance at being a sword for the death of crucifixion?

That doesn't sound nearly as fun. What changed between Gideon's time and ours? Sadly for men everywhere, there aren't nearly as many swords in the New Testament. One of the only ones that does make an appearance Jesus tells Peter to put away, and then he undoes the work it has just done (Luke 22:49-51). I don't know if I want to be *that* sword for the Lord!

I don't think there's anything intrinsic to pacifism that makes one manly, though. What Jesus was getting at with Peter was that he needed to lay down his own will. Peter probably still wanted a military Messiah, and Jesus was asking him to sacrifice that dream. Even though he didn't understand yet that Jesus would be crucified, this was his opportunity to be crucified with Christ, to die to his own way and live for Jesus' way (a lesson Peter learned by the end of his life). Jesus was about to show him the ultimate example of manhood, not by winning a glorious military victory but by dying to save his friends.

Even in the world of the swordsman, the value of a noble death can be appreciated. Just think of all those movies again: "noble deaths" would have been another acceptable answer for a common theme. I won't list them because I don't want to spoil the films for any who haven't had the chance to experience them (If you haven't, I recommend them all, despite one needlessly inappropriate scene in *Braveheart*, some truly atrocious acting in *Star Wars*, and the flawed adaptation of *Lord of the Rings!*), but why are these moments in fiction so powerful? Could it be that they resonate with us so strongly because they mirror the greatest story of manhood ever? Jesus, the pinnacle of humanity, the quintessential man, died fighting for his friends. Is that what manhood is all about?

Jesus told Peter to put away the sword because he knew the cross was his mission. He also knew he could avoid the cross, but he chose to endure it anyway (Matthew 26:52-54). In willingly laying down his human will and even his earthly life for the good of others, he gave us the pattern to follow to become men and women of God. It's not about us. It's about living life completely surrendered to the will of God.

I should have quoted the whole of Galatians 2:20 earlier: "I have been crucified with Christ and I no longer live, *but* Christ lives in me. The life I live in the body, I live by faith in the Son of God, who loved me and gave himself for me." See how Paul sets Jesus as the example? We live by faith in him—the one who loved us and gave everything for us. And oh by the way, he didn't stay dead. God raised him back to life, showing us what kind of glory also awaits us on the other side of this fleeting earthly life if we'll give everything to follow him. He lives *in us*, Paul says. So why are we afraid of dying?

What if we lived like *Gladiator*? The movie shows how the condemned fighters had to greet Caesar as they entered the arena with the words "Those who are about to die salute you." They knew they were going to die, and so they fought with abandon. There's no point in leaving anything in the tank when any day or moment could be your last. Only by fighting with all the life and strength they had would they last another day. Now, death might not be so imminent for us, but in the larger picture aren't we all "those who are about to die"? We have no idea when it might happen, so why not live like we have nothing to lose?

That must be the place Gideon and his fighters got to. I mean, I don't doubt that they believed Gideon when he told them that God would give them the victory, but I don't think they went into battle on blind faith either. It was still 300 guys against tens of thousands. They all had to be thinking there was a very high likelihood of their death regardless of the ultimate outcome. They just realized they would rather face certain death than see their families and their nation continue going through the torture of foreign occupation and persecution. In dying to themselves in this way, they came alive to accomplish the victory. They're the ones who came up with the idea of the sword for the Lord. And now it's in the Bible!

That reminds me—there is one good sword in the New Testament. It is the Sword of the Spirit, also known as the Word of God. In case you wanted any more proof that swords are manly, this is the same sword that Jesus, the perfect example of manhood, now has *coming out of his mouth*! His glory is now so strong and imposing that the very manly apostle John (who, by the way, had already been through multiple failed execution attempts because Jesus wouldn't let him be killed before he finished talking to him) fell down like a dead man when he saw it. If you don't think a sword coming out of someone's mouth is powerful, there's something wrong. Read the description of Jesus in Revelation 1 and just try to convince yourself you wouldn't have done exactly what John did. It's that intense.

Jesus said himself that he came not to bring peace but a sword (Matthew 10:34). That Sword of the Spirit, the only weapon in the armor of God (Ephesians 6), is the same one we carry with us in the words of Christ. He knew that his words were powerful and his claims would cause division. He also knew that those who truly live like he did and say what he said might face a literal sword. That's why he said in the same discussion that we lose our lives by trying to save them, and only by willingly losing our lives for Jesus can we find them. Only when we die can we truly live.

So maybe we aren't exactly like the gladiators. They were about to die, but we are already dead—crucified with Christ. They were condemned, but in Christ there is **no** condemnation for us. As we are crucified with him, we are reborn as sons and daughters of the Almighty—walking in his protection and favor, bearing his power and showing his righteousness to the world. Only in realizing we are dead and coming alive in Christ can we become the men and women God wants us to be: the ones who wield the (s)word of the Lord against the lies and darkness of this age; the ones who humble themselves in order to glorify God; the ones who embrace Jesus' mission of loving the world, teaching people to know him and telling everyone how much he loves them.

After all, what good is even the sharpest sword if our battle is not against flesh and blood, but against the powers of darkness in an evil age? God would have to give us quite an otherworldly sword to cut through that!

He did. "The weapons we fight with are not the weapons of the world. On the contrary, they have divine power to demolish strongholds" (2 Corinthians 10:4). What are the strongholds of the enemy around you? Addiction, depression, human trafficking, racism, materialism? If you're looking for the magic bullet, the weapon that can bring down even these giants in the land, look no further. It's you.

It's the Spirit of God in you, his sons and daughters. It's His Spirit in all of us. His love and grace give us power together to sever the chains that keep us bound in childish ways and to set free more voices to add to the shout of praise, more sword-sharpened lives cutting through the darkness to reveal His wonderful light.

In the end, the great longing of manhood is not to find our own way. It is to be a weapon in the hands of the Master. But it's more personal and relational than that metaphor implies as well. As we're sharpened, each of us becomes not just a sword but also a son, walking in the full power and love of our mighty Father for his great deeds of mercy and justice on this earth, bringing him glory and enjoying his presence all the way. This is my cry. This is our cry. This is Gideon's cry.

Lord, would you give us the grace and strength to live this way? Amen.

Epilogue

Maybe you thought that by the end of this book, I would tell you exactly how to be a man. Honestly, I kind of thought that by the time I had written it, I might actually figure manhood out. I haven't. But I have started walking in my identity as a son, and I never want to stop. God's call to manhood is more alive in me than ever, and I grow into it more every day, yet it's more about his love and favor than about anything I do.

I wrote all this with a few hopes in mind. First, I want all of you who are trying to grow up into men and women of God to know that someone else is walking this road too. It's not just me, either; it's a whole generation of us. There's great camaraderie in that. Just know that you aren't going crazy if you have dreams too big to fit into the system you see around you. The truth is that the system is too small, not the dreams too big. Maybe you'll meet resistance; Gideon did too (see Judges 8). Most things worth doing are strongly resisted by someone, and we have a real enemy. God, though, is God of the impossible, and he might want to glorify himself by having you do something crazy like Gideon did. If so, he'll make it work.

Second, I don't want any of you to feel ashamed of where you are. Maybe you're like me, with a numerical age you feel should be accompanied by having life a bit more figured out than you do. May I suggest that where you start and where you are now are both fairly insignificant compared with where you're facing? Gideon's initial cry was little more than a pathetic whine, but God turned it into a shout for his glory as Gideon looked to him! All I know is that there's no power or benefit in feeling ashamed. If there's one thing I've learned manhood is *not* about, it would be looking at ourselves all the time. If you look to God, you'll find a much better view: "those who look to him are radiant; their faces are never covered with shame" (Psalm 34:5).

Third and probably most important, I wrote this as a story and not a manifesto because I don't think manhood or anything else this side of heaven is about arriving. It's about *walking*. I don't know if we ever fully get there, but I do know we get stronger, we learn lessons that are important enough to pass along, and we get to know the One we're walking with. True manhood can't be about what we accomplish; rather, it's about who goes with us and how he changes us on the way. That also means there's no room for coasting. Even Gideon stumbled a bit once he thought his mission was complete! You can only coast downhill, but the call to walk with Jesus is ever upward (Philippians 3:12-16).

Becoming a man just isn't a one-time deal like I was hoping. There's no time we can point to and say that's where it happened. But I have a feeling that, if we keep walking with God, we'll see when Jesus completes us at the end of the road that he did most of the work long before. He wants us to do justice, love mercy and walk humbly with him (Micah 6:8). Every time we fight for those who need help, learn to accept and enjoy God's grace, and just walk and talk with God, manhood happens. We may not feel it happening, but it does. I take the walking part quite literally these days: I just go on long walks talking with God. It often doesn't seem like anything changes, but later on I find that God has given me exactly what I need for the upcoming challenges when I walk like this.

Now you know some of my story. What's yours? Don't stop here. Yesterday's inspiration is not enough for tomorrow. Keep looking to God, worshiping him, loving him and growing into the man or woman he calls you to be and you long to become. Keep cutting through the darkness. Answer Gideon's cry to live as a sword for the Lord, and see what stories you walk into!

ABOUT THE AUTHOR

Ben Barnhart is a pastor, writer and editor from Cleveland, Ohio, who is experiencing more and more of the blessing and manhood he was longing for as he wrote this book. Now a husband to his beautiful bride, Liz, and a father to their son, Ezra, he is excited to pursue all that manhood and a life of worship have to offer in a new season. You can contact him or join the discussion by telling part of your own story of growing up at facebook.com/gideonscrybook

19264478R00119

Made in the USA
Lexington, KY
28 November 2018